I wish you ~~had~~ the ~~[barcode]~~
Can Handle
Capt. Ed Hughes

Toys are "U"
Fish are "me"
Captain John Cochran

El Commodoro,
Here's to many days of fishing the North East. When I get my first fleet of Boats I expect you to do the printing for my staffs shirts!
Thanks see you soon
Chris

The
Orvis Guide
to
Saltwater
Fly Fishing

The Orvis Guide to Saltwater Fly Fishing

NICK CURCIONE

Lyons & Burford, Publishers

Design by Daniel J. McClain

Printed in the United States of America

10 9 8 7 6 5 4 3 2

———————————————————

Library of Congress Cataloging-in-Publication Data
Curcione, Nick.
The Orvis guide to saltwater fly fishing / Nick Curcione.
        p.   cm.
Includes bibliographical references and index.
ISBN 1-55821-252-3
1. Saltwater fly fishing.   I. Title.
SH456.2.C87   1994
799.1'6—dc20   93-44243
                                    CIP

Contents

Foreword

NICK CURCIONE always reminds me of a bumblebee in a jar. He is in constant motion, and his agile mind is always seeking fresh ideas, especially if they are related to fly fishing. He has been using a fly rod for all the years I've known him, and no one seems to enjoy the sport more than Nick does. Fly fishing is a true passion for him.

Nick was born and raised in the East and began his fishing career there. But he has lived for many years in California, where he has chased every saltwater species along the West Coast and down into the Sea of Cortez. He has spent considerable time fishing in many foreign waters, too. There are a lot of tarpon and some sailfish in Costa Rica, for example, that were "sore-mouthed" by Nick. He is a master of the lead-core shooting head, as well as a great caster and fish-fighter.

Nick's approach to fishing has always been a practical one and this book is filled with practical hints on how you can become a better fly fisherman. This is not a book of tales about his and his friends' accomplishments. Instead, it is a common-sense approach (and common sense isn't too common these days) as to what tackle is needed, where to go, and how to catch various saltwater species.

The information is all first hand, gained by Nick's on-the-water experience. If you want to learn the fascinating sport of saltwater fly fishing, or improve your techniques in this area, this book will prove invaluable.

Tight lines, but—not too tight!

—Lefty Kreh

Introduction

As A SEMI-LANDLOCKED lad growing up in and about the shadows of New York City in the 1950s I spent a good deal of the idle time forced on me by poor weather and lack of funds leafing through the pages of fishing magazines that I acquired by a variety of means, both fair and foul.

However, playing on my fascination with tales of high seas adventure that depicted dramatic struggles with the world's great gamefish, an aunt who was a librarian lured me to the works of writers like Zane Grey and Ernest Hemingway; here I gained a jump on most of my literary-impoverished street-urchin peers, whose reading interests seldom wandered beyond the realm of comics. The truth of such tales notwithstanding, given my social circumstances, the prospect of my ever engaging in such pursuits seemed as likely as enticing a mako with a muddler—so I relegated such dreams to the realm of fantasy.

Instead, I contented myself with occasional outings on Long Island Sound with my free-spirited jazz-musician uncle who loved the fresh air, sunshine and saltwater. For him, catching fish—primarily flounder and porgies—was purely incidental, but for me it was everything and only years later did I come to appreciate the other qualities that go with being out on the water.

The tackle set-up (it seems hardly worthy of that designation) was an object lesson in simplicity, the age-old handline. I didn't know or much less care about its role in the history of fishing. In terms of modern technological standards it was primitive. Beyond that it was functional; even more importantly, it was fun. By holding the line across your palm and fingers the dynamics of the strike is translated directly to your hand; the sensation never ceases to light up my emotional circuits. The transmission is direct and instantaneous. This may seem like a radical transition but it is the sensation of the strike telegraphed directly to your hand that remains for me one of the principal attractions of fly fishing. Rod Harrison, the great Aussie long rodder who can turn a phrase about as well as he turns those magnificent gamefish he battles down under, characterizes the sport as "Fishing with a handline that you can cast with a rod."

For some that kind of thinking may take out too much of the mystique, but Rod is absolutely correct. It wasn't until I actually began catching fish with fly gear that I realized I was reliving many of those same boyhood experiences I had enjoyed with the handline. Of course, aside from the fact that in fly fishing one limits oneself to artificials only, the most dramatic difference lies in the fact that the line must be cast, and this is what initially attracted me to the sport.

It was on Long Island Sound, where I started fishing as a kid, that I first encountered saltwater fly rodders casting poppers to bluefish tearing up terrified pods of baitfish on the surface. This was in 1970 and fishing was by then very much a part of my life. In my early teens I moved to Southern California with my parents and spent over a dozen great years fishing local southland and Mexican waters. I returned to the East Coast in 1970 to assume a teaching position at the City University of New York but I had no intentions of retiring my fishing gear.

I became friends with Dick Alley, a writer in Connecticut, and one day he invited me out in his skiff to chase bluefish. He had a fly outfit on board but I didn't give it much notice because he was content to let me have at them with my spinning gear. Before long we pulled up on a big school that was being worked over by a couple of boats. What fascinated me more than the surface commotion was the fact that the guys in these skiffs were using fly rods. As it turned out, they were friends of Dick's and all belonged to the Connecticut Saltwater Fly Rodders. I was so taken with the beauty of the casts, not to mention the explosive strikes on the poppers, that I knew then and there that this was a sport I had to learn. I only remained in the East for three years but they were some of the best times of my life. The Connecticut bunch were the nicest people you could ever meet and I established some lifelong friendships. They also knew their fly fishing and I learned a great deal from them.

Lou Tabory, one of the best fly casters in the country, spent countless hours teaching me the basics. (He also took the time to review portions of this manuscript.) John Posh, who is now the proud owner of a successful tackle shop in Stratford, Connecticut, introduced me to the art of fly tying. It was his intimate knowledge of local conditions that enabled me to take my first fly-rod striper on a homely creation he showed me how to tie.

During this period I also had the good fortune to meet and become close friends with two of the superstars of the sport, Lefty Kreh and Mark Sosin. The experience was like a high-school quarterback being coached by Joe Montana. Even though we had only recently met, Lefty (who was living in Miami at the time) was gracious enough to loan a few of us his Hewes Bonefisher to fish the Florida Keys. It was my "baptism by fire"; now there was little doubt as to my life's consuming passion.

In 1973 I returned to Southern California where I connected with other fly-fishing luminaries like the late Myron Gregory, Harry Kime, and Dan Blanton. All three are pioneers in the history of West Coast fly fishing. Myron, a champion-calibre caster, was instrumental in having the American Fishing Tackle Manufacturers Association (AFTMA) adopt a standardized numerical system to designate fly-line weights. Harry was the first to explore Baja waters carefully with the fly rod and he was making sinking lines with powdered lead long before they were commercially available from major manufacturers. Dan Blanton does it all—and he does it extremely well. He's a world-class caster, an innovative fly tyer (his Whistler series is terrific), and a spectacular fisherman. Danny was primarily responsible for getting me into sinking lines and shooting heads.

Ed Ow, who was publishing *Angler* Magazine at the time, got my writing career off the ground; this gave me a chance to meet other fly-fishing greats like Bill Barnes, Billy Pate, Bob Stearns, Stu Apte, and Chico Fernandez. I first met Bill Barnes on a writing assignment in Costa Rica; Bill owns and operates the world-famous Casa Mar fishing lodge, which has been the scene of some of the most memorable fishing experiences of my life. Ed Rice, who puts on the International Sportsmen Expos, gave me the opportunities to learn and share with other luminaries in the sport—like Stu Apte, Bob Popovics, and Ray Beadle.

For the knowledge and experience I gained from these greats, I'll always remain deeply indebted. But more importantly are the friendships that have been forged with all those who share the same passion for this sport. As evidenced by the growing numbers who are attracted to fly fishing, and increasingly to the saltwater brand, this is no longer an exclusive fraternity—nor should it be. I hope that in some small way this book will help broaden its horizons.

Quite unexpectedly, the impetus for this book came from Tom Rosenbauer last spring while I was rowing him around in King Harbor in search of bonito. He knew I was planning a manuscript on saltwater fly fishing and asked if I would be interested in writing a handbook for Orvis. Needless to say, it is an honor to offer such a work under the auspices of Orvis, one of the most respected names in fly fishing. In addition to Bill Barnes, Lou Tabory, and Rick Ruoff—who all offered valuable insights on various fisheries covered in this book—I want to offer special thanks to Bob Jones and Lefty Kreh for their editorial assistance on an early draft of the manuscript.

There are five main chapters. Chapter 1 is designed to familiarize you with the basic tackle systems, lines, leaders, knots, and flies. Chapter 2 is devoted to fly casting, an integral part of the sport and something that you will have to learn by doing. Chapter 3 covers basic techniques, from retrieving line to fish-fighting strategies. Chapter 4 is a rather long section because it takes up the very diverse subject of coastal fishing. The latest frontier in saltwater fly fishing is the offshore grounds and this is treated in Chapter 5.

I hope you find this book helpful.

The Orvis
Saltwater Advisory Team

IN THE SPRING OF 1992, I was asked to become a member of the newly formed Orvis Saltwater Advisory Team. The chance to join forces with some of the country's top saltwater fly fishermen was one offer I couldn't refuse.

Steve Huff and Rick Ruoff from the Florida Keys, Lou Tabory from the Northeast, Paul Bruun from the Rocky Mountains (he has a wealth of experience in both fresh and saltwater), and I (representing the West Coast) have all been afforded the opportunity to work both individually and collectively in the design, development, and refinement of the full complement of Orvis products directed to saltwater fly fishing.

As Orvis's affable president, Perk Perkins, stated: "This is quite a break with anything we've done in the past. We've always relied on an in-house staff of experts that includes at least twenty-five world-class fly fishermen, our field representatives, and our dealers for input on products. But while our staff may only spend one hundred days a year fishing in saltwater, this new team is collectively on the water over seven hundred days a year. They *live* saltwater fly fishing and with their input, we feel confident that we'll have the best-conceived, best-tested gear money can buy."

If you have used any of Orvis's recent saltwater fly tackle and related equipment, I'm sure you'll agree that Perk's objectives are fast becoming a reality and the reason for this is twofold. First, in addition to the Perkins brothers (Perk and Dave) they have the top people in each of their respective areas: Tom Rosenbauer, Randy Carlson, Howard Steere,

Jim LePage, Tom McMillen, Joe Dion, and Matt Glerum, to mention a few. These guys love their work and it shows. Second, under Perk's "green light"-style management system, Orvis is a company that listens. Fresh ideas and innovations are encouraged and you'll see that reflected in products that range from an MIT-engineered stripping basket to the exclusive Floating Tip fly line that is the brainchild of Lou Tabory.

Throughout the book I'll be referring to a number of these products, most of which in some way or another the advisory team has had a hand in or, as the case may be, even a foot.

Some of us are fortunate enough to spend a great deal of time on the water, but like most anglers, all of us on the advisory team regard our fishing time as precious. And to help maximize that experience for everyone who loves the sport, we and the rest of the folks at Orvis are committed to providing the best in fly-fishing tackle and related equipment. I hope that in the pages that follow you will glean information on tackle and technique that will help you derive maximum satisfaction every time you venture into salt water.

The
Orvis Guide
to
Saltwater
Fly Fishing

1

The Fly-Tackle System

FLY FISHING AS DISTINCT FROM OTHER MODES OF ANGLING

IN THE INTRODUCTION I noted that as sophisticated and complex as some may like to portray it, fly fishing is closely akin to more primitive forms of angling. The simple handline is still the principal mode of fishing in many parts of the world, and since handlining doesn't use a reel to manipulate or cast the line, it bears a much closer resemblance to fly fishing than it does to conventional or spinning tackle.

The major difference between fly-fishing gear and other types of tackle is the method of presenting or casting the offering to the fish. The objective of all rod-and-reel systems is to present a bait or lure to the fish with the line serving as the connecting link between the hook and the angler. In fly fishing, the heavy line carries the offering to the fish; the nearly weightless fly is just along for the ride. In contrast, with conventional and spinning tackle it is the heavier bait or lure that transports the comparatively weightless monofilament or Dacron line.

This fact brings up two additional differences between the three types of tackle. In order to cast with conventional or spinning gear, you need something with weight at the end of the line. But in fly fishing, because it is the weighted line that carries the fly, a heavy or wind-resistant fly will actually make casting more difficult. A fly line with nothing attached to it except a leader is relatively easy to cast. In freshwater fly fishing, where the flies are often imitations of tiny insects, the effect of the fly on casting is negligible. Frequently, however, this is not the case in saltwater, where the flies are often designed to simulate different kinds of baitfish. They tend to be considerably larger and their size and weight can upset the aerodynamics of the fly line.

The second difference between fly tackle and the other two systems is that in the former the reel is not used to cast the line. There is no free-spool mechanism or its equivalent on a fly reel. In all three systems the rod plays a key role in propelling the offering, but only with conventional and spinning outfits does the reel play an integral part in the process.

A reel is unnecessary to cast a fly, and in many distance-casting tournaments all the line is carefully coiled at the caster's feet and the rod is used sans reel. Even in many freshwater situations, the fly reel serves as little more than a storage receptacle for the line. When fish aren't large or strong enough to run off a lot of line, they can be played by the hand-stripping technique often practiced with trout, bass, and panfish. There are also times in saltwater when this is a useful strategy, but more often you'll encounter strong-running fish that will make off with all the fly line and then start taking out backing from the reel's spool. This is when a good drag mechanism comes into play, and we'll discuss this feature shortly.

A fly reel is also out of the picture when retrieving the line after a cast. Instead of winding the line onto the reel, the fly is retrieved by pulling (stripping) the line in by hand.

FLY LINES

NOT ONLY IS THE fly line the principal item that distinguishes fly fishing from other methods of angling, it is also the single most important component in the fly fisherman's tackle system. You can be an expert caster and deliver the most appealing flies imaginable, but it all goes for naught if you're not putting the offering where the fish are. While there are certainly other factors in the equation, it is the fly line that governs the distance and depth at which you will be able to fish.

As one example of this, let me relate an incident that took place some years ago when I made a trip back East to fish with some of my buddies in Connecticut. I had become very familiar with sinking lines and shooting heads and I was anxious to share my knowledge with my friends. The initial reception my lines received was considerably less than enthusiastic. This type of reaction is often part of a general pattern that many of us are guilty of from time to time: a tendency to shy away from innovation. The "tried and true" certainly have their place. But bear in mind that much of what is accepted as standard practice today is the product of someone's willingness to strike out anew and try something different.

The breakthrough for my Connecticut buddies came one night when we went wading for stripers. After hearing that the bass would be feeding sub-surface, I inquired as to why everyone was using full-floating lines. My friends felt that their weighted streamers and four-and-a-half-foot leaders would be sufficient to put their flies within the stripers' feeding zone. But since we faced a moderately strong current on the incoming tide and some pockets that were twelve to fifteen feet deep, I opted for a lead-core shooting head. Some of the guys shook their heads in outright disagreement, while a few were genuinely interested in how I would fare.

In the first half-hour of casting all I managed were two snags. No one else caught any fish either, but I was reminded that I was the only one to hang up on the bottom. Shortly thereafter, my line went taut and I thought for a moment that I was snagged once again. But when the line started to slip from my tightly clenched fingers, I knew that I was on to a nice fish.

There's something special about catching fish from shore, especially on a fly rod, and after a few minutes of exhilarating striper-struggle I was clutching a bass in the ten-pound class. That night I managed to catch one more of about eight pounds before we had to call it quits. Some of the more skeptical attributed my success to pure luck. Others wanted to learn more about this line that could shoot a fly with the speed of a clay pigeon and that sank like a shot-put in sludge.

By itself, the fact of catching a couple of stripers when everyone else went fishless may not mean very much. But seeing this experience repeated many times over in widely different locales on different species can only lead to the conclusion that one's choice of fly line is absolutely critical to one's success. Just as a golfer has to have a working knowledge of the various clubs that are used during the course of a game, the fly rodder should at least be acquainted with the basic characteristics and functions of the different fly lines currently available.

The shape of the fly line, referred to as its taper, determines its casting characteristics. There are four basic types: level, double-taper, weight-forward, and the shooting head or shooting taper.

As its name implies, the level line has no taper. Its diameter is uniform along is entire length. Instead of serving as a casting line, it is better used as a running or shooting line behind a shooting head; more about this later. Again, as the name indicates, the double-taper line is tapered at both ends. Some dry-fly aficionados prefer it for delicacy of presentation, but for most applications in fresh and saltwater, the weight-forward taper is a better choice.

Just like some of the people who pose for dieting ads, the taper of a weight-forward line is such that most of the line's weight (measured in grains) is concentrated up front. Most weight-forward lines are about ninety-feet long, with a sixty-foot section of relatively thin running line behind a heavier thirty-foot "belly" or "head." The line is designed to be cast with the heavier section outside the rod tip. At the end of the power stroke on the forward cast, this front section will sail out in a tight loop, pulling the running line with it. We'll look at this in more detail in Chapter 2.

A direct offshoot of the weight-forward line is the shooting taper or shooting head. Essentially, a shooting taper consists of the first thirty feet of a weight-forward line joined to a very thin running or shooting line that is often 100 feet long. The longer running line is necessary because one of the primary functions of a shooting head is to let you achieve greater casting distance. In fact, shooting tapers were developed out on the West Coast by salmon and steelhead fishermen who had to cast their flies into football-field-wide rivers.

Shooting tapers are among the most useful lines for saltwater fly fishing. Unlike most freshwater angling, distance is often a critical factor in the salt. You're almost always fishing great expanses of water. The farther you can cast, the more water you can cover, and this often spells the difference between success and failure. Furthermore, the elements in a marine environment are often much less favorable than they are on inland waterways. It is a rare day on the ocean when the wind doesn't blow, and a shooting taper is much more effective under these conditions. Just as with a weight-forward line, the final forward cast with a shooting taper is made with the heavy thirty-foot section outside the rod tip. But because the running line is thinner than that of a one-piece line, it's more easily pulled along and this makes for greater distance.

In addition to various weights, lengths, and tapers, fly lines are also available in different densities. The basic distinction is between floating and sinking lines, but thanks to today's technology, when it comes to the latter you can buy lines with many different sink rates. Some sink slowly, some do so at a moderate rate, and others are designed to go down like rocks. Floating lines are best when you are fishing shallow flats, and they are also used for special applications such as casting surface poppers. There's no doubt that surface action makes for some of the most exciting episodes in fishing; just the sight of breaking fish is enough to get most anglers pumped up. Most saltwater action, however, takes place somewhere below the surface. Given the nature of fly lines, fly fishermen can easily enjoy both worlds. Fly lines are weighed in grains, not ounces. This means that even a comparatively dense line, such as a lead-core shooting head, is not going to plunge into the depths as quickly as a lead sinker or metal jig. If fish are busting the surface and all you have is a sinking line, you can still get in on the action. All you need do is begin retrieving line as soon as the fly hits the water. The line sinks slowly enough so the fly will run only a few feet below the surface. This effect can be enhanced by using unweighted flies tied with feathers, hair, and other materials that add to a fly's buoyancy.

When the fish are holding relatively deep, even if you're using a fly line that carries a designation like the Orvis Extra Fast Sinking, you have to exercise a little patience. This may take the form of a "countdown method," which entails exactly what the term implies. If you are not sure exactly where the fish are holding, you may have to try various depths until you finally hit the productive zone. For example, on a trip off Isla Cerralvo at Baja's East Cape, I used a lead-core shooting head to get my fly to the schools of yellowfin tuna that the guide assured me were concentrated somewhere in the depths below us. It took about five casts before I drew the first strike. After each cast I allowed the line to sink progressively deeper, slowly making a mental count as it did so. Finally, when I got to a count of fifty on the fifth try, I began stripping and was struck almost immediately.

Every fly line can be divided into two parts: core and coating. By modifying these parts, lines can be designed with specific performance features that meet the needs of nearly any situation or special condition.

The core of a fly line is responsible for its tensile strength. Every fly line is built to be much stronger than the heaviest tippet normally used with that line. For example, a 2- or 3-weight line will test out at about eighteen pounds, while the heaviest tippet used with such a line should be around 6-pound test. As you go higher up the line-weight scale, the strength of the core increases proportionately. The construction and physical characteristics of the core material also have an impact on line performance. For example, by using a stiffer braided-monofilament core material, it's possible to make lines that are stiffer and that shoot better.

The coating is what gives a line its mass (weight). By modifying the coating and regulating how it is distributed along the length of the core, it's possible to dictate how a line performs: its relationship of power to delicacy, how high it will float or how quickly it will sink, its shootability, its durability, and more. Every fly line has a taper design, determined by how the coating is shaped and distributed along the line. The weight-forward design can serve as an example. Nearly all WF lines have the sections shown in the accompanying illustration. Here is what each one does:

Tip: A short six- to twelve-inch level section to which the leader is attached. This section's role is to protect the line's taper. *Front Taper*: This is the section of the line that determines how delicately or powerfully the fly is delivered. Typically four to eight feet long, it gradually decreases in diameter from the belly section out to the tip. This graduation of the line's mass (weight) determines its ability to transfer your casting energy. *Belly*: This large-diameter section is where most of the weight of a line is located and, consequently, where your casting energy is carried. *Rear Taper*: Gradually decreasing in diameter from the thicker belly section to the much thinner running line, the rear taper creates the transition so important for casting smoothness and control.

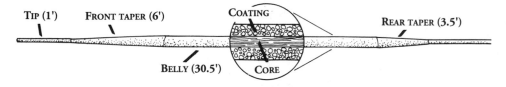

TIP (1')   FRONT TAPER (6')   COATING   REAR TAPER (3.5')

BELLY (30.5')   CORE

Anatomy of a Typical Weight-Forward Fly Line

Running Line: This exists primarily to make distance casting easier. The running lines on WF lines are small in diameter, creating little resistance and friction when shooting line. They are also light, an important factor in shootability because the momentum and mass of the portion of line moving through the air must pull the running line out through the guides. *Head*: This part is really the combination of front taper, belly, and rear taper. Shooting tapers are short lines consisting only of the first thirty feet or so of a WF line, and must be attached to a separate shooting line in order to be used.

The performance advantages of one line over another are primarily the result of modifications in one or more of these areas: taper design, coating formulation, and the characteristics of the core material. In this respect, nearly all Orvis lines have unique tapers and/or coatings that set them apart from others on the market. Of special interest to saltwater fly fishermen are the Lead Core Shooting Heads, HY-FLOTE lines, Density-Compensated sinking lines, Mini Sink Tip lines, Braided Mono Core lines, HLS lines, and the Floating Tip sinking lines. All these lines have the exclusive Orvis braided loop that makes changing leaders as simple as unlocking loops; you don't have to cut anything to replace a leader.

The Lead Core Heads are designed for rod weights 7 through 12. When you want to get the fly down in a hurry, these are the lines to use. For other subsurface applications, look to the Density-Compensated lines. The Class III sinks approximately three inches per second, while the Class V plummets twice as fast—about six inches per second. "Density compensation" refers to the fact that these lines remain straight as they sink, instead of sinking belly-first. Of course, there are situations where you want the fly to sink, but not in such a way that it is likely to snag on a structure-ridden bottom. This is when Lou Tabory's floating-tip concept comes into play. The Orvis Floating Tip line combines a ten-foot HY-FLOTE tip with a Class III sinking section. This enables you to present a fly subsurface in the fish's feeding zone without the hassle of constantly hanging up on obstacles such as grass, kelp, or rocks.

Another very versatile fly line in the dual-density category is the Mini Sink Tip, which consists of a HY-FLOTE main line with a four-foot Class V sinking tip. The relatively short sinking tip makes it easy to pick the line up off the water to begin the next cast.

In really hot-weather conditions that can make conventional fly lines feel like overcooked linguini, the Braided Mono Core lines are the way to go. Featuring a special Tropic Taper in conjunction with a stiff braided-monofilament core, these lines shoot much better than conventional Dacron-core lines.

Since their inception, shooting heads have always been equated with distance casting. But when you have to make "downtown" presentations, don't overlook the HLS series of lines. These are long-distance lines. The 8-, 9-, and 10-weight lines are 100 feet long with 52-foot head sections that make it easy to carry a lot of line in the air.

With a selection like this, it's possible to cover any situation you're likely to encounter in saltwater.

BALANCING YOUR TACKLE

BEFORE DISCUSSING THE DIFFERENT methods used to connect a shooting taper to a running line, a few words on properly matching fly lines to rods are in order. Balanced tackle is something to be strived for no matter how you fish, but it is especially critical where fly-fishing tackle is concerned. With conventional and spinning rods, all top-name manufacturers designate the specific line and lure weights that each of their sticks is designed to accommodate. The same is true for fly rods, except for two differences. Obviously, lure weights are not relevant, and, when referring to line, the weight designation refers not to its breaking strength but to its actual weight. Fly-line weights are measured in grains. Thanks largely to the efforts of the late Myron Gregory, the American Fishing Tackle Manufacturers Association has established numerical designations to refer to the various grain-weights of fly lines. An 8-weight line, for example, weighs approximately 210 grains, a 10-weight about 280, and a 12-weight about 380.

The weight designation is written on a line's box and spool, but there is no numbering on the line itself. After you start accumulating lines you will have trouble identifying their weights if you haven't worked out some type of labeling system. The easiest way was shown to me by Lefty Kreh years ago. Simply take a waterproof pen and mark the tag end of the fly line with a series of slashes to designate its weight. A half-inch-long slash could indicate 5 (you will seldom use a line lighter

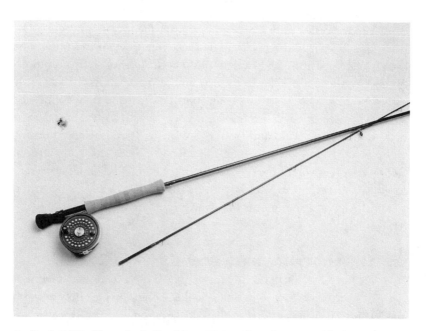

An Orvis SaltRodder rod—built with an HLS medium-fast-action blank—is an excellent choice for many saltwater fly-fishing occasions. *Photo courtesy Orvis.*

than this in saltwater), while a short mark stands for a 1. Therefore, one long slash followed by three short marks would designate a line as an 8-weight. Two long slashes will tell you it's a number 10. If you follow this system every time you get a new line you will save yourself a lot of headaches trying to figure out which line is which.

To be able to cast effectively, you must match a rod with a line of the proper weight. Ideally, if you are using a rod with a 10-weight rating you would match it with a 10-weight fly line. A proper match is especially important for those who are just beginning to learn to cast; novices often experience unnecessary difficulties because they use mismatched rod-and-line combinations. As you become more accomplished you can alter these combinations to suit your own needs. Nowadays, most good fly rods will handle line weights that vary from their specific ratings. For example, an 8-weight rod might comfortably accommodate a 9- or even 10-weight line.

Unless you are after large gamefish over the fifty-pound mark, 8-, 9-, and 10-weight outfits will handle most conditions in saltwater. Just by way of comparison, an 8-weight outfit is the type of setup commonly used by those who like to fly fish for freshwater bass. In fact, it is sometimes referred to as a "bass bug" outfit. Under the right conditions it could be used on species as diverse as bonefish and striped bass. When there is little or no wind and the flies are small, 5- and 6-weight outfits will provide great sport on strong fish such as bonito and baby tarpon. But on the other end of the scale, there may be times when it's necessary to go to a 12-weight to wrestle with fish that may weigh less than ten pounds. A good fisherman is one who can adjust to the conditions at hand.

USEFUL KNOTS FOR SALTWATER FLY FISHING

WHEN YOU THINK ABOUT it, it's impossible to use a fishing line without tying some kind of knot in it. So if the line is the vital link between you and the fish, it's only as good as the knots you tie in it. But it's also important to use premium-grade line.

After two full years of testing and revising formulas, Orvis has made available a leader material that I feel is ideal for saltwater fly fishing. Appropriately, it is labeled Big Game Super Tough, and having fished it under conditions ranging from the coral flats of Christmas Island to the bluewater grounds off Costa Rica, I've found that it does indeed live up to its name. In addition to high knot strength, a key quality that tippet material should incorporate for saltwater use is abrasion resistance, and this line certainly has it. This is an International Game Fish Association "class" line, which means that the labeled breaking strength is absolutely true to what is actually measured in breaking tests. So, for example, if you are interested in trying for a 16-pound class-tippet record, and you are using a Big Game Super Tough Tippet designated at 16-pound test, you can be sure that it will test out at that rating.

If you consult a dictionary, you'll see a number of definitions for the word knot. The one we want to avoid speaks of "difficulty or problem." Although some may seem so at first, most of the knots fly fishermen use are not especially difficult to tie, and when done correctly they eliminate all kinds of problems. Without getting too specific, my Webster's defines a knot as an interlacement of the parts of a flexible body such as cordage or line. What this simply means is that a section of line is laid back on itself in a series of turns or twists. Since this is the case, some weakening of the line is almost inevitable. The trick is to try to tie knots that will yield 100 percent of the breaking strength of the unknotted line. This is important in all types of fishing, but it is especially critical in fly fishing. First of all, fly fishing is basically light-tackle fishing. Because the breaking strength of the leader is not very much to begin with (if you follow IGFA guidelines, the heaviest class tippet is only 20-pound test), it stands to reason that you want to get the absolute maximum out of the line you are using. Knots that substantially weaken a light line's breaking strength will put you at a great disadvantage. You have already limited yourself by using relatively light tackle; you don't want to handicap yourself any further by tying inferior connections that make the link even more tenuous.

Second, as a saltwater fly fisherman you will find yourself making connections between lines that differ greatly in diameter and breaking strength. There are any number of times when it is necessary to use a heavy shock leader to withstand abrasion from a fish's teeth, gill plates, scales, or any structure that may be in the area you are fishing. It is not uncommon to tie an 8- to 20-pound-test class tippet to a shock leader that may test as high as 80 or 100 pounds. Since the class tippet is the weak link in the system, the object is to utilize a connection that will at least yield the full breaking strength of this section of leader.

As the term implies, knot strength refers to the breaking strength of a line with a knot tied in it. In a heavy shock tippet, a knot that significantly weakens the line may not pose much of a problem because its higher breaking strength is still considerably greater than that of the lighter class tippet. A simple overhand knot, for example, is referred to as a "cutting knot" because when it is tightened that is precisely the effect it has on the line, and the line's original breaking strength can be reduced by as much as fifty percent. If you tied such a knot in a 100-pound test shock leader that was connected to a class tippet of, say, 16-pound test, there would be no problem because even with its strength reduced to half (50-pound test) the shock tippet is still much stronger than the 16-pound test line. But tie an overhand knot in the 16-pound leader and you'll probably find that you won't be landing many fish. The point is that you want to attain the full measure of breaking strength in the lightest section of your leader system.

One of the best knots you can tie for this purpose is the Bimini Twist, or, as it is sometimes called, the twenty-times-around knot. The Bimini looks a lot more complicated than it really is. Unfortunately, many people are put off by this knot either because they did not receive proper instruction or they did not bother to practice. You don't have to have the dexterity of a surgeon, but tying it does take a "feel" and this will come with a little practice. Even though this is probably the most involved of all the knots that you will need to know, I am starting out with it because it forms the very basis of your leader system. The double line or loop produced by a Bimini is used to make any number of different connections that are important in building a leader system. Many of the line connections in fly fishing are made via a loop-to-loop setup that makes line and leader changes a simple matter of either locking or unlocking lines with end loops in them. The strongest loop is formed by means of the Bimini. Even when I'm not using a shock leader, I still employ a Bimini as part of my leader system. Admittedly, the best way to learn this knot is through personal instruction, but the following steps will help get you started. Just don't be intimidated; I have taught hundreds of people how to tie it.

Another excellent knot for creating a double line loop is the Australian Braid. Like the Bimini, it yields 100-percent knot strength and serves all the same applications. But the Braid has the additional advantage of providing a cushioning effect when the line is under pressure. You can demonstrate this yourself by tying both knots in two identical leader sections and subjecting each to a simple stress test. Taking one at

Bimini Twist

Form a loop in the line, place your hand inside the bottom portion of the loop, and begin to rotate it 20 turns to form a series of twists.

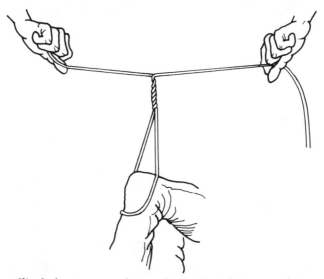

Slip the loop over your knee and spread both hands apart to force the twists together.

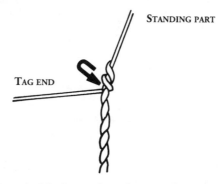

STANDING PART

TAG END

Position the tag end of the line so that it forms a right angle to the twists. Pull slightly upward on the standing part of the line so that the tag end will begin to roll over the column of twists.

Continue to make a series of close, barrel-type wraps over entire column of twists.

(figure continued on next page)

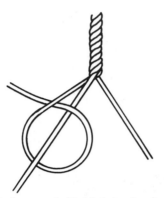

With the wraps held tightly in place between your thumb and index finger, make a half hitch around the left leg of the loop with the tag end—and then pull it up tight.

Take the tag end and make 4 or 5 turns over both legs of the loop, working back toward the bottom of the column of barrel wraps.

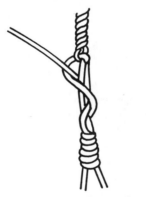

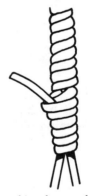

Pull the tag end slowly, forcing the spirals to bunch up tightly.

Snug everything down and trim the tag end.

a time, grasp one end in your right hand and the other in your left and slowly pull your hands apart. You will notice that the Braid knot, unlike the Bimini, will stretch a little under pressure and then return to its more compact configuration when the pressure is relaxed. This is the cushioning effect and the added insurance it provides when exerting maximum pressure against a big fish is worth the little extra time it takes to tie this knot.

After hundreds of trials, I have found that tying the Braid with a small Bimini as the foundation results in the strongest connection.

The Bimini (or Australian) Braid

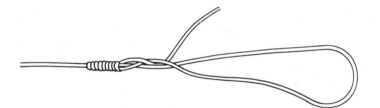

Begin this knot by tying a 10-turn Bimini and securing it with a single half hitch.

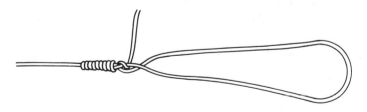

Pass the tag end over and around the right leg of the Bimini Loop.

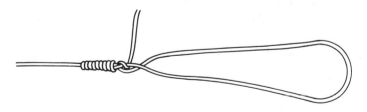

Pull the tag end through the loop and snug it up against the juncture of the braid.

(figure continued on next page)

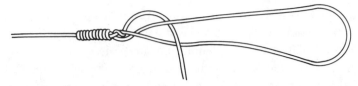

Repeat this process over and around the left leg of the Bimini Loop.

Continue the braid for a minimum of 15 turns around each leg of the Bimini Loop.

Pinch the last braid between your thumb and forefinger and finish off the knot the same way you did the Bimini.

The finished knot should look like this.

In tying the fly to a shock leader or directly to the tag end of the class tippet there are two basic options that will determine how the fly will ride during the retrieve. One method allows the fly to swing on an end loop; the other is where the knot is snugged down tight against the hook eye.

There are a number of knots used to form end loops and they vary significantly in their breaking strength, so you want to be careful in selecting which one to use. When a fly is tied to a heavy shock tippet, the knot's breaking strength generally is of little concern simply because the shock tippet's higher breaking strength is normally more than enough to offset any weakening effects of the knot. This of course assumes that the knot system used to join the class tippet to the shock leader is one that does not compromise the tippet's rated break-strength. That is why the Bimini is so important, and we will shortly see how it is used to make connections between the class tippet and shock leader.

One popular knot for creating an end loop for the fly to swing on is the Uni Knot. Unlike other loop knots, this is a slip-knot, which means that under pressure it will slide down and snug itself against the hook eye.

The Uni-Knot

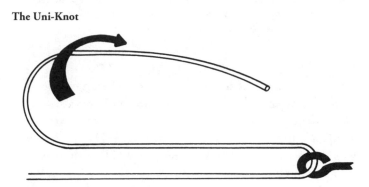

Pass the line through the eye of the hook and bring the tag end back about six inches so that it lies parallel to the main section of the line. Form the loop as shown.

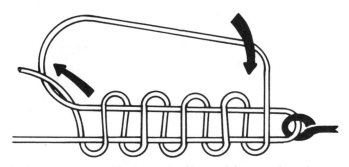

Take 4 or 5 turns around both strands of line and then pass the end out through the loop.

(figure continued on next page)

Pull on the tag end to snug up the wraps.

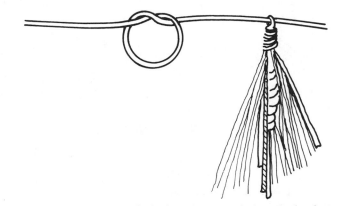

Pulling on the standing part of the line will cause the loop to become smaller and eventually slide up against the eye of the hook. Therefore, continue pulling just to the point where you have the desired loop size. Then tighten it again by pulling on the tag end.

Another good knot that makes for an end loop for the fly to ride on is a modification of the time-honored Bowline Knot used by boaters. This knot was first shown to me by a guide at Casa Mar named Clifford; in his honor I simply refer to it as Clifford's Knot. Harry Kime, who had the good fortune to spend entire seasons at the lodge fishing nothing but tarpon, used this knot almost exclusively for tying his flies to 100-pound shock leaders.

Clifford's Knot

Tie an Overhand Knot in the leader approximately 6 or 7 inches from the tag end and then pass it through the eye of the hook.

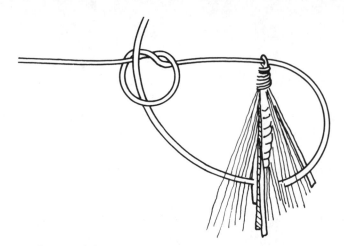

Pass the tag end through the center of the Overhand Knot.

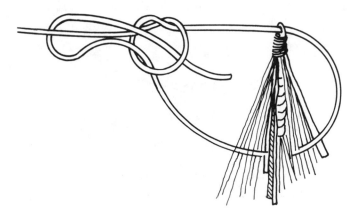

Pass the tag end behind and around the standing part and re-enter the Overhand Knot.

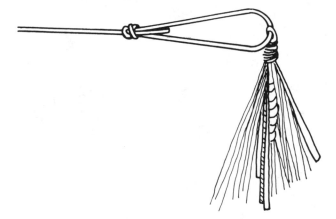

Tighten the loop by grasping the fly in one hand and pulling on the standing part of the leader with the other hand.

When tied correctly, the tag end will slant downward toward the hook eye. This is one of the advantages of this knot because there is less chance for debris to foul on the tag end when it faces opposite the direction the fly is pulled in. Another neat feature of this knot is that it is often possible to untie by working the tag end back up through the overhand circle. You can change flies without having to cut or change the leader.

Neither of these end loop knots offers high break strength (remember, this isn't a problem with heavy shock leaders) but one that does is the non-slip mono loop, which I believe was first illustrated in *Practical Fishing Knots II* by Lefty Kreh and Mark Sosin.

Non-Slip Mono Loop

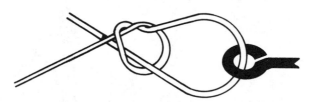

Tie an Overhand Knot and pass the tag end through the hook eye and back through the Overhand.

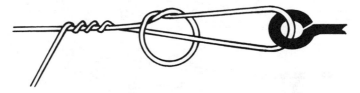

Make a series of wraps around the standing part.

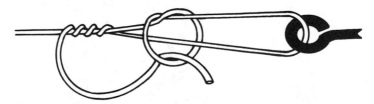

Pass the tag end back through the Overhand Knot.

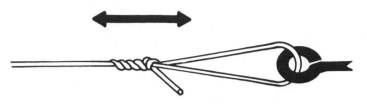

Pull slowly on the tag end to begin tightening the wraps. To seat the
wraps firmly, pull the standing part and the fly in opposite directions.

For tying the fly snug against the line, one of the all-time best connections is the Trilene Knot. Properly tied, it will yield 100 percent of the
line's rated breaking strength. Although this is a simple knot to tie, you
have to take care in the process of drawing it up properly before tightening it. As with all knots tied in monofilament line, moistening it with
saliva prior to tightening acts as a lubricant that helps create a good snug
connection.

Trilene Knot

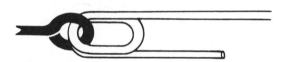

Pass the tag end through the eye of the hook twice.

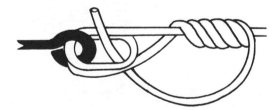

Make five wraps around the standing part and bring the tag end back
through the double loop.

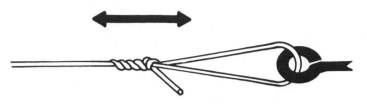

Begin tightening by alternatively pulling on the standing part and the tag
end. Snug the knot tight by pulling on the tag end.

The Haywire Twist and the Albright, both of which are used for connections involving wire, will be taken up in the section on leaders.

No book on fly fishing would be complete without mentioning the Nail Knot. It is used primarily for joining the butt section to the fly line when a more or less permanent connection is desired. However, as I learned from Bob Stearns many years ago, it can also be used to fashion an end loop in the fly line. To do this quickly and easily, a modification in the original knot, appropriately called the Speed Nail Knot, is used. To tie it you should use a sewing needle, but in a pinch I've gotten by with a fairly small-diameter, stiff piece of mono or a toothpick. Here's how I join a butt section to the tag end of a fly line.

The Speed Nail Knot

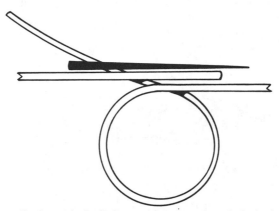

Lay a needle alongside the fly line and form a circle with the leader, one end facing right and the other left.

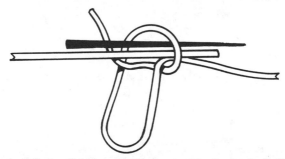

Take the right leg of the loop and begin wrapping it over the fly line, needle, and leader; be sure to work to the left.

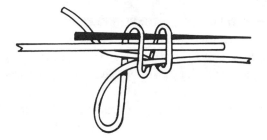

Make the wraps parallel to each other.

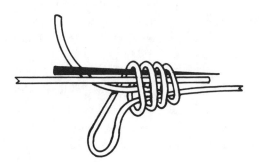

Make 7 or 8 wraps.

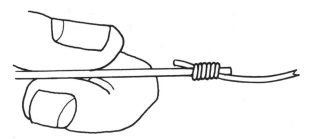

Begin to tighten the wraps by pulling on the part of the leader extending out toward the tag end of the fly line.

Finish tightening by pulling on both ends of the leader.

JOINING THE RUNNING LINE TO THE SHOOTING HEAD

THUS FAR WE HAVE established that the major difference between a weight-forward line and a shooting-head system is that the former is one single, continuous section of the line while the latter consists of two separate lines (the thirty-foot head and a hundred feet or so of running line) that are joined together. The two important considerations to be reckoned with here are the choice of running line and the methods by which it is connected to the shooting-head section.

We'd all love a perfect running line, one that would never foul! Well, there isn't one. Some perform better than others, all have their drawbacks. You basically have three choices: fly lines that are specially designed as running lines, hollow-core braided dacron, and monofilament.

Orvis has an exclusive HY-FLOTE running line that's designed to repel water. This is an important characteristic; by shedding water, the line will remain free of minute particles of grit or silt. In time, the effect of stripping a line coated with grit is like running an emery board across your fingers. This doesn't do the rod guides any good, either. Second, the high-visibility chartreuse allows you to see the HY-FLOTE line in the water easily. Unless you are trying to fish very deep (fifty feet down or more) in strong current, the fact that the line floats does not significantly impede the fly's descent.

If you build your leaders according to IGFA specifications, then the heaviest class tippet will not be more than 20-pound test. Obviously, regardless of the running line you choose, always make sure that its breaking strength greatly exceeds that of your class tippet.

For a quality of smoothness that's as slick as silk across your fingers, you can't beat monofilament as a running line. This, coupled with its relatively small diameter, makes it ideally suited for long-distance casting. But it too is not without fault. First, because it is lighter than conventional lines, it is more prone to being buffeted about by the wind and this can cause some maddening tangles. Also, some of these lines have too much stretch, making it difficult to set the hook; this can be a major drawback on hard-mouthed species like tarpon and wahoo. Mono is also more prone to abrasion than coated lines so you constantly have to check for wear. To offset some of these problems, at least partially, for saltwater use a monofilament running line should be in the

40-pound-test range. This relatively large diameter makes the line easier to use in the wind and gives added insurance against abrasion. Be sure to stretch these lines before casting; otherwise you'll have bothersome coils that will continue to foul.

One of the principal advantages in using a hollow-core braided mono for a running line is that it is possible to make connections that are almost as smooth as a single, continuous section of fly line. For years I have been testing a variety of these lines; the best I've found for these purposes is Orvis's Orange Braided Mono Running line. The diameter is large enough to resist being buffeted easily by the wind; and, compared to other lines I've used, it is much less prone to tangles. On the other hand, the line is not so bulky that it takes up an unreasonable amount of space on the reel spool. The orange color aids visibility, which can be an advantage in monitoring the line's position in the water when fighting a fish. Finally, the line has loops spliced in both ends; this enables you to make quick, interchangeable connections with different shooting heads.

If, however, you prefer one continuous connection between the shooting head and running line, the modification is relatively easy. First, cut the loop from the braided line. Then slice the tag end of the head on a bias and work about three to four inches of it inside the core of the braided mono. The trick here is to cause the braid to flare out slightly so that it will slide over the fly line. To effect this, slowly work the braid over the line by alternately pushing it (this will cause it to bulge) and then pulling the tag end (this tightens the braid by flattening the bulge). During the process a few strands of the braid at the tag end will separate but these can be secured after the shooting head is inserted into the braid the desired distance. It's a simple matter of wrapping over the loose ends with fly-tying thread and a bobbin. After everything is securely bound, to make sure the thread will not unravel, the wraps should be completed and tied off by means of a whip finish.

This is the same procedure rod builders use to finish wrapping guides to a blank. Take a piece of 8-pound-test mono and fold it over itself to form a loop about four inches long. Tie a double Overhand Knot in the tag end to secure the loop. This will serve as your whip-finishing tool (loops of dental floss may also be used). When the loose ends of the braid are bound securely with the thread, lay the mono loop parallel to the line. Approximately at the mid-point of the loop, begin rotating the bobbin around both the loop and the line. Wind the thread toward the "U" end of the mono loop, making a series of ten to fifteen tight, barrel wraps. Pinch the last wrap against the line and loop with your thumb and forefinger. Cut the thread from the bobbin and insert the tag end through the mono loop. Grasp the knotted end of the loop and pull it out from under the wraps, drawing the tag end of the thread with it. This draws the thread under the wraps. Pull on the tag end to make sure everything is tight and then cut the thread close to where it exits from under the wraps.

Once the shooting head has been worked into the braid and the loose ends firmly bound together, you have a connection that works on the principle of the Chinese two-finger braid game you may have played as a kid. Pulling the shooting head and braided running line in opposite directions causes the braid to tighten around the shooting head. The result is a strong, smooth connection.

Joining a Braided Mono Running Line to a Shooting Head

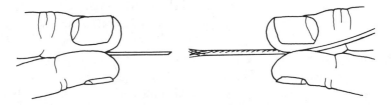

Cut the tag end of the shooting head on an angle.

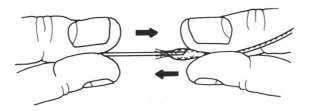

Insert the tag end of the shooting head into the braid.
Flare out the braid to help accommodate the shooting head.

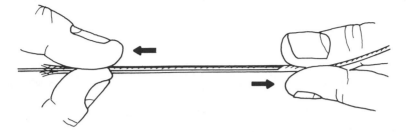

Work approximately 3 to 4 inches of the shooting head into the braid.

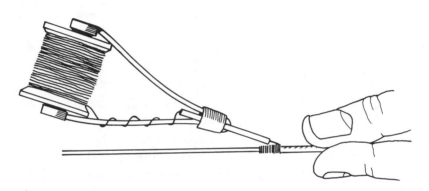

Using fly-tying thread and a bobbin, wrap over the strands of braid that have separated. Whip finish the wraps and coat the knot with a rubber-base cement.

When you use monofilament as a running line you are limited to tying some type of knot to make the connection to the shooting head. If you want a more or less permanent connection, use a Nail Knot to connect the mono to the shooting head. The connection can be smoothed over with a few applications of rubber cement. You can also whip finish over the knot with fly-tying thread; any time you do this, though, apply some type of rubber cement to protect the threads.

Since a shooting head is only thirty feet long, one advantage to this system is that you can change lines relatively quickly. But to effect this you must use some sort of loop-to-loop connection. That means that a loop will have to be fastened in both the shooting head and running line—except, perhaps, when you're using monofilament running lines.

Interlocking Loops

WHEN INTERLOCKING LOOPS, BE SURE THEY LAY FLAT, LIKE THIS . . .

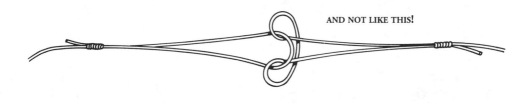

AND NOT LIKE THIS!

With a loop in the end of the shooting head, it's often practical to simply tie the mono directly to the loop using a three-and-a-half-turn Clinch Knot. Compared to fly line, mono is inexpensive so when you want to change shooting heads merely clip the mono at the knot. This only involves a few inches of line; you will want to discard the running line long before you have cut away a significant portion. Of course, a loop can always be tied in the mono by means of a Surgeon's Knot or Bimini Twist. After trimming these knots, a small nub of mono usually remains and this might catch on the guides. To make the connection as smooth as possible, take a pair of pliers, mash the remaining tag end flat, and whip finish it with fly-tying thread and a bobbin.

End Loop in Mono Running Line

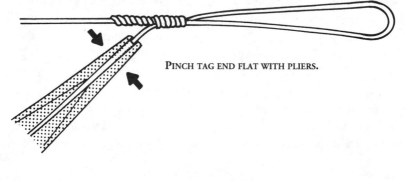

PINCH TAG END FLAT WITH PLIERS.

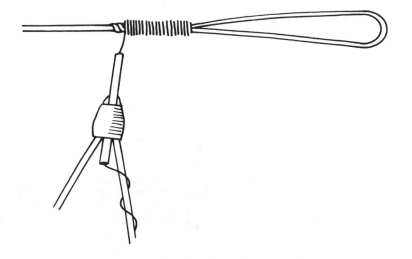

Of the various ways to fasten a loop in a shooting head, one I learned from Lefty Kreh is one of the most secure. You don't have to be a tailor, but this does involve a little sewing (at least five stitches). This method is often used to join two lines in one continuous section but with a slight modification it makes an end loop that's virtually inseparable. First, strip about four-and-a-half inches of coating from the fly line (soaking the line in Acetone for a few seconds softens the finish and makes it easy to strip off the finish). This is accomplished by taking a piece of twenty-pound dacron, tying it around the fly line by means of a Girth Hitch, and jerking it out away from the line. The finish will come off clean, exposing the dacron core. Double this core section back over itself to form the desired loop and stitch the two overlapping sections together with size "A" fly-tying thread. Double the thread before stitching. End loops in level fly lines used as running lines are fashioned in the same manner. In either case, the stitching should always be whip finished with fly-tying thread and then coated with a few light applications of rubber cement.

Stitched End Loop

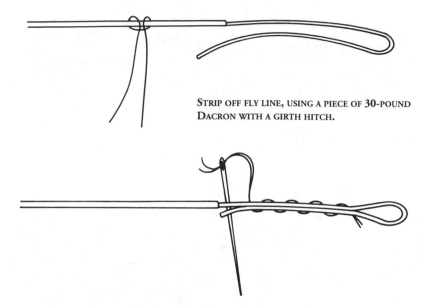

STRIP OFF FLY LINE, USING A PIECE OF **30**-POUND
DACRON WITH A GIRTH HITCH.

If you want to forgo the tailoring operation, another good method of fastening a loop in the end of a fly line is to use a length of hollow-core dacron braid. The process is essentially the same as the one used for joining a shooting head to a hollow-core dacron running line. The only added step involves forming a loop in the hollow-core braid. Since you will be making a splice, you will need a tool to feed the line back into itself. A fifteen-inch length of #2 or #3 stainless-steel trolling wire is ideal. Fold it in half at its mid-section and be sure to make a sharp bend so that it will pass easily into the braid's hollow core. Sewing needles can also be used. Try to obtain one about two and a half inches long with an eye that is large enough to accommodate the dacron braid.

To insure a sufficient length of braid to form a splice, and still have enough braid remaining to work over the tag end of the fly line, you should cut a section approximately twenty inches long. This will yield a loop with a diameter roughly the size of a quarter and still leave enough braid to slip over three or four inches of fly line. (To form a loop large enough to pass over a fly reel naturally requires a longer section of dacron.)

Begin by threading approximately six inches of the dacron braid through the eye of the needle. Then form the desired loop size by positioning the needle eye back down along the standing part of the dacron. At this juncture, insert the needle point into the braid. Carefully work the full length of the needle (two-and-a-half inches) down inside the core.

Once the needle is completely inside the braid, push the point out through the line. With the needle outside the line, gently pull on the six-inch strand that was originally passed through the needle eye. This tag end should slide through the hollow core of the braid and exit at the juncture where the needle point was pushed out through the line. At this point you'll want to snug down the braid. Simply insert your finger in the loop, grasp the standing part of the line with your other hand, and steadily pull your hands apart.

Even though the splice is nice and tight, to prevent the loop from pulling loose you should make a second splice. Insert the needle (with the accompanying tag end protruding through the needle eye) back into the standing part of the braid about one-quarter inch from the point where it was pushed out. Work the needle down through the standing part for a distance of approximately one-and-one-quarter inches (half the length of the needle) and then push it out through the braid. Pull everything tight again and trim the remaining tag end flush to the standing part. If there is s small remaining nub it can be smoothed over by whip finishing with a bobbin and fly-tying thread. Now join the remaining part of the braid to the tag end of the fly line, following the method described for attaching a hollow-core running line to a shooting head. Be sure to whip finish the frayed end of the dacron braid where the fly line was first pushed through.

Fastening an End Loop in Hollow Core Line

Thread the braid approximately 6 inches through the eye of a needle.
(figure continued on next page)

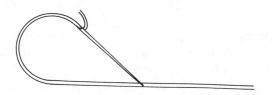

Position the eye of the needle back over the standing part of the braid to form a loop approximately the size of a quarter.

Insert the needle at this juncture and work it into the core of the braid.

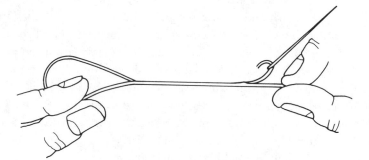

Work the full length of the needle (about 2-1/2 inches) inside the braid, then push it out with the tag end still protruding through the eye of the needle.

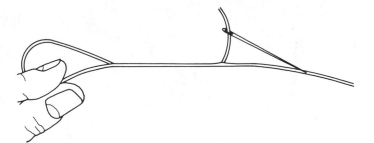

Pull the splice tight by inserting a finger in the loop and pulling on the standing part in opposite directions.

To prevent the splice from coming loose, make a second splice by inserting the needle back into the standing part 1 inch from the point where it was pushed out. Work the needle inside the braid approximately 1-1/4 inches and then push it out.

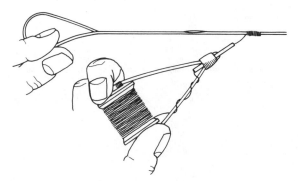

Trim the remaining tag end flush to the standing part. If a small nub remains, whip finish it with a fly-tying bobbin.

Fastening a loop in the end of a leadcore shooting head is quick and easy, especially if you are using an uncoated line. Pushing back on the dacron will expose the core of lead. Work the dacron back about five inches and break off the lead. Next, fold the hollow dacron back over itself to form the desired loop and tie a double Overhand Knot. You can do exactly that same thing when joining a length of hollow-core braid to the tag end of a fly line. Instead of splicing in a loop, simply tie one by means of double Overhand Knot. Though this is not quite as smooth as a spliced loop, it should still pass through the rod guides without any difficulty.

Finally, an end loop can be fashioned in a fly line using the Speed Nail Knot previously described. Fold the fly line back on itself to form the desired loop. Lay a needle alongside the doubled section at the base of the loop. Now take about a foot-long piece of 12- to 15-pound-test mono and make the same series of wraps. In this case you will also want

Forming an End Loop in the Fly Line By Means of Two Speed Nail Knots

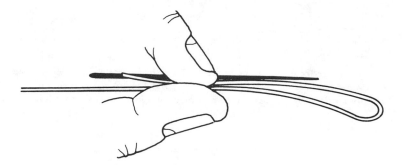

Fold the fly line back on itself to form the desired loop and lay a needle along-side the doubled section.

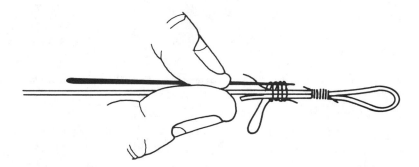

Take a 12-inch section of 12-pound-test mono and tie two Speed Nail Knots.

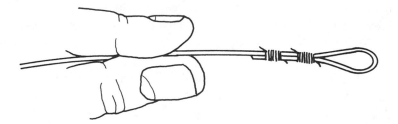

Trim the ends of the mono close to the wraps and coat with rubber cement.

the mono to imbed itself in the fly line's coating; due to its small diameter, the mono will do this with little difficulty. The only difference here is that this mono is not serving as a leader, so after snugging it tight, you should trim both ends close to the wraps. For added security I make a second Nail Knot right behind the first. Coat the mono wraps with rubber cement and you will have a finished loop that is at least as strong as the fly line.

The object in all this is to have a connection that is at least as strong as the lines themselves, with a minimum of bulk and a smooth finish that will flow through the guides effortlessly. Since many of these operations are time-consuming, they obviously should be completed before you venture out on the water. Fortunately, for those of you who have neither the time nor the inclination to fasten these connections, Orvis's pre-looped fly lines, shooting heads, and braided running line are a great convenience.

BACKING

SINCE MOST SALTWATER FISH have a penchant for going "downtown" when they feel a hook, you will need more line than the fly line and running line. This additional line is the backing, and it is most often dacron, a soft, braided synthetic line. Approximately two hundred yards of 20- to 30-pound-test backing will be sufficient for most inshore conditions. For bluewater brutes like tuna and sharks you'll want at least two hundred and fifty yards, preferably of 30-pound-test backing. There are some who opt for the light 20-pound because they can pack more of it on the reel, but I recommend the 30-pound test for added insurance. A 20-pound-test class tippet does not leave much room for error if the 20-pound backing gets nicked or abraded in some way. If the backing breaks, you will part company with your entire fly line. This can even happen with 30-pound test, as I sadly experienced after a four-hour battle with what may well have been a world-record yellowfin on fly. (The present record is the outstanding catch of an eighty-one pounder by Jim Lopez back in 1973.) If anything was to break it should have been the sixteen-pound-test IGFA class tippet. Instead, the backing broke and it was brand new from a high-quality manufacturer. Apparently it had a weak spot.

When fighting big fish, Orvis's Quick-Sight Fluorescent Backing is handy—especially for the skipper who has to maneuver the boat—because the line is so highly visible. It's also flat, which makes it pack nicely on the spool of the reel.

One of the best and easiest ways of connecting the backing to the spool is by means of a four-to-six-turn Uni Knot. To connect the backing to a fly line or running line you can use a loop-to-loop system. Tie a Bimini in the tag end of the dacron and loop this to a loop that is fastened in the spool end of the fly line.

THE LEADER SYSTEM

THERE ARE THREE TYPES of tippet sections that may be incorporated into a leader system. Appropriately named, the butt section is the section of leader that is attached to the end of the fly line. Generally, it is either 25 or 30-pound test. The next section of leader is called the class tippet and it is the weakest part of the system. For record purposes the IGFA has established six classes: 2, 4, 8, 12, 16 and 20-pound test. To conform to IGFA standards this section must be at least fifteen inches in length from knot to knot. Where there is a likelihood of having the line cut or abraded by a fish's teeth, gill plate, or whatever, a shock leader is joined to the class tippet with the fly tied to the tag end of the leader. This may be either monofilament or wire, but for IGFA consideration it cannot exceed twelve inches including the knot used in making the connection to the class tippet.

Saltwater fish become skittish when they are in shallow water, usually less than six feet or so. The classic example of this would be the Florida Keys and Caribbean flats. Here you need finesse, because the slightest disturbance—such as the line slapping the water—can scatter the fish like a depth charge dropped in an aquarium.

The three leader systems I'm about to describe are ones that I learned from Lefty. As he advised, I use the loop-to-loop systems for practically all the connections. The first leader system is for shallow water conditions. A four-foot section of 25- to 30-pound-test mono serves as a butt section, and is looped to the end loop in the fly line. This is followed by a three-foot section of 20 pound, two feet of 15 pound, and a two-foot length of class tippet generally from 12 to 4-pound test. The fly is tied directly to the end of this section. The beauty of this system is that

A Typical Saltwater Leader

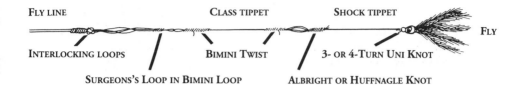

FLY LINE   CLASS TIPPET   SHOCK TIPPET

FLY

INTERLOCKING LOOPS   BIMINI TWIST   3- OR 4-TURN UNI KNOT

SURGEONS'S LOOP IN BIMINI LOOP   ALBRIGHT OR HUFFNAGLE KNOT

changes in the length of the leader can be made simply by making one section longer or shorter. You don't have to re-rig the entire leader.

The two other leader systems are basically the same except for the butt section and the addition of a shock leader. In situations when fish aren't particularly wary and you want to go deep, it's often best to eliminate the butt section and join the class tippet directly to the fly line. Tie a Bimini Twist in one end of the tippet, double the resulting loop over itself, and tie a double Overhand Knot (Surgeon's Loop). This loop now has two strands of line and is interconnected with the end loop in the tag end of the fly line.

The third type of leader incorporates a shock leader. Here you tie a second Bimini Twist in the other end of the class tippet and use the resulting loop to make the connection to the shock leader.

To join the class tippet to the shock leader there are a variety of connections that may be used, but the best and easiest to tie was shown to me years ago by a guide in Casa Mar. Lefty calls it the Huffnagle Knot.

Huffnagle Knot

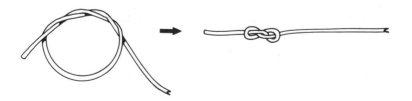

Tie a double Overhand Knot in the shock leader and snug it down slightly.

(figure continued on next page)

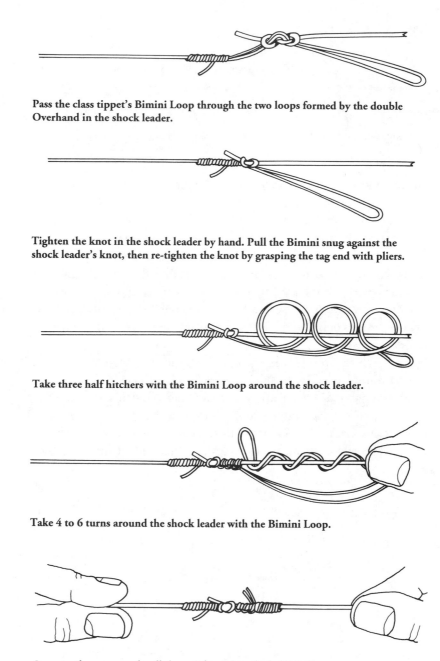

Pass the class tippet's Bimini Loop through the two loops formed by the double Overhand in the shock leader.

Tighten the knot in the shock leader by hand. Pull the Bimini snug against the shock leader's knot, then re-tighten the knot by grasping the tag end with pliers.

Take three half hitchers with the Bimini Loop around the shock leader.

Take 4 to 6 turns around the shock leader with the Bimini Loop.

Snug up the wraps and pull them tight against the half hitches.

A knot that some prefer to the Huffnagle is the Albright. It remains one of the best connections I know of for joining mono to wire. This is not a particularly difficult knot to tie but you have to be careful when drawing it up tight. It is tied as follows:

Albright Knot

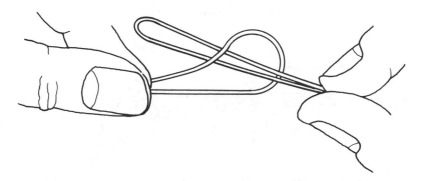

Form a loop in the leader material and push the tag end or the class tippet's Bimini Loop through this loop.

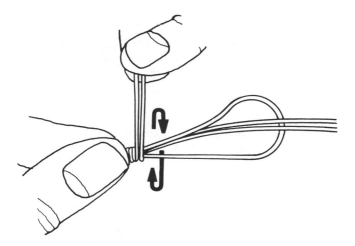

Take the tag end of the Bimini and make 8 to 10 wraps around the double section of the leader, working from left to right.

(figure continued on next page)

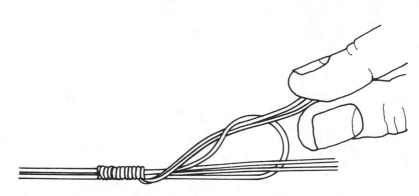

After the last wrap, insert the Bimini's tag end out through the leader's loop.

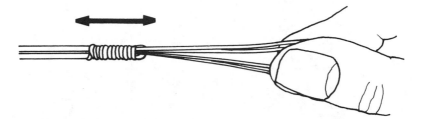

Begin tightening by alternately pulling on the tag end of the Bimini and the standing part of the leader.

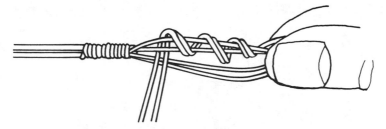

Take 3 turns around the standing part of the Doubled Bimini, working from right to left. Bring the Bimini's tag end through the belly that has been formed.

Gradually snug up the wraps.

Tighten the wraps and trim the tag ends.

Regardless of whether you use the Huffnagle or the Albright, with the Bimini knots properly tied, you can be sure that you will achieve 100 percent of the rated breaking strength of the lightest line (class tippet) in your leader system.

To join single-strand wire to the fly's hook eye, the Haywire Twist is best. When tying this connection be sure to make three and a half true "X" wraps in the wire before starting the barrel wraps. If you merely wrap one leg of the wire around the other without forming a criss-crossed "X," under enough tension the wraps can pull loose.

Haywire Twist

First criss-cross the wire.

Be sure to form a true "X".

(figure continued on next page)

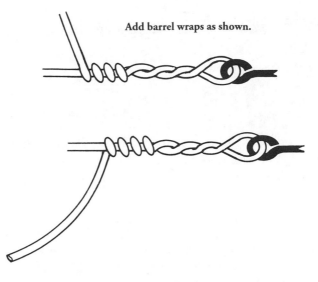

Add barrel wraps as shown.

Provide a "crank handle." Bend the handle opposite the wraps and the wire should break off cleanly.

Wire shock leaders (dark-colored) are an absolute must for wahoo, king mackerel, sharks, and the barracuda found in the tropics. As a rule of thumb it's best to use the smallest diameter possible. I try not to use leader heavier than about 55-pound test and I don't use more than about four inches or the fly will not turn over properly on the cast. One exception to using the short wire leader is fishing sharks in deep water where they are being chummed to the boat. Basically, all you are doing is laying the fly out on the water in the chum slick. Since there is little if any casting and retrieving, you can use a full twelve-inch wire shock leader.

FLY RODS

THE FLY ROD, MORE than any other item of tackle, represents a compromise of different functions. Unlike the case of, say, a big-game rod used for trolling or bait fishing where its sole purpose is to fight fish, a fly rod, even those at the heavy end of the scale, must also serve as a casting tool. If you can't cast with it, it's not going to do you much good. But on the other hand, you don't want a rod that doesn't have the backbone to pump fish out of the depths. Fortunately, leading manufacturers today

A Power Matrix-10 rod. *Photo courtesy Orvis.*

are apprised of all the requirements and build their rods accordingly. So all I'll mention here are some general features that you should look for in a saltwater fly rod.

First, as far as materials are concerned, for all practical purposes you can forget about bamboo. These rods just are not designed for a marine environment. There are some top-quality glass rods on the market but most serious anglers now opt for graphite. This material has come a long way since it was first introduced into the fishing-rod industry; rods like Orvis's latest Power Matrix-10 are truly state of the art. When you consider the demands made on saltwater fly rods, it's no exaggeration to describe them as engineering marvels. Just a few years back you had to sacrifice either casting or fish-fighting ability; today it's possible to have both in one rod.

I am no engineer and won't pretend otherwise. But, like the other members of the Saltwater Advisory Team, I do know when a rod has excellent casting and fishing qualities and these rods excel in both categories. All of us on the team have been closely involved in the design and testing of the Power Matrix series, but it was Howard Steere, the quiet master rodbuilder, who began to use a new, high-strength, high-modulus graphite/resin matrix that results in a blank that is 30 percent tougher than other sanded rods. There is more graphite in the tip to give added strength to this critical area, yet the tip section has a 10 percent smaller diameter than previous rods. Likewise, the ferrule is 40 percent smaller in diameter and 30 percent shorter, which makes it significantly lighter but with no sacrifice in strength.

But a rod blank is only part of the picture. You also have to make sure that the hardware, like guides and reel seats, is of top quality. Anything less will inevitably be relegated to the junk pile when exposed to the ravages of a saltwater environment. With this in mind, Howard saw to it that the Orvis saltwater rods came equipped with silicon carbide stripping guides and hard chrome-plated stainless-steel snake guides. There is an extra-large tip top to facilitate the free flow of knotted connections.

The reel seats are black anodized high-tensile-strength aluminum. The hood and sliding cap are fitted with Delrin inserts to grip the reel foot securely and help prevent corrosion. The two locking rings have an O-ring between them to insure positive locking and easy dismantling of the reel. And because saltwater gamefish can require prolonged fighting times, the fighting butt features a comfortable, non-slip molded rubber cap.

In terms of fly rod length, the choice is much narrower than that for conventional and spinning rods. Ideal lengths for most saltwater applications are generally nine feet. There are some slightly longer models, like nine-and-a-half-footers that are useful in situations when it's advantageous to hold longer sections of line outside the rod tip—when wading a shoreline, for example—but by far the sticks that get the most use are the nine-footers.

I do not like a keeper ring on my saltwater fly rods. When battling large fish it is common practice to pull on the rod above the handle and the keeper ring can be a definite bother. Since this is also the consensus of the other Saltwater Advisory Team members, you won't find keeper rings on Orvis saltwater fly rods. Instead, it's more efficient just to hang the fly on a snake guide. In fact, a convenient way to store and transport a rigged outfit is to pull line out from the rod tip, loop it around the reel, and then hang the fly on the fourth or fifth snake guide down from the rod tip. Take the section of line extending from the tip and wrap it around the rod twice, catching it on one of the large stripping guides. You can now store and transport several outfits together without the lines tangling on each other. This system also allows you to get back into the action fairly quickly because you already have a good length of line outside the rod tip, and probably the entire leader. Unwrap the line from the snake guide and rod, strip out more line from the reel in preparation for your cast, unhook the fly from the snake guide, and begin your presentation.

More so than with other types of rods, fly rods are meant to be cast. This means that they must be comfortable; a critical part of the rod is thus the handle or grip. Unless the anatomy of your hand is truly unique, you'll find that the half or full-wells grip is the most comfortable.

Finally, keep in mind that, like everything from golf clubs to cameras, a fly rod is only as good as the person using it. Learning to be a good caster takes practice; someone who is less than proficient will not suddenly attain perfection just because he has a great rod in his hands. We'll take this up in the next chapter.

REELS

LEFTY KREH, IN *Fly Fishing in Saltwater*, states that: "No saltwater fly fishing equipment is as important to success as the reel. Many modern-day catches would be impossible on the reels designed for freshwater fishing." For saltwater work, the fly reel must do more than simply store line. In addition to being able to stand up to the rigors of a marine environment, a critical feature of any fly reel designed for saltwater is its drag system.

Even in its heavier models, in comparison to other saltwater tackle systems, fly gear would still have to be considered as light tackle. In fact, I'll explore in Chapter 3, dealing with fish-fighting techniques, one of the tricks that skilled light-tackle anglers use when battling big fish; they set a light drag, often of only a pound or less, and then apply additional pressure manually.

Even though you may be intent upon catching one particular species, in saltwater the neighborhoods are often very mixed and you never know when some really bad critter—one you haven't anticipated—will come along and take your fly. When this happens, you'll want to have adequate gear—and a vital part of that is a reel with an adequate drag system.

It isn't necessary to have a very expensive reel every time you venture into saltwater but it is necessary to have a well-designed reel. (In fact, there are kinds of saltwater fishing, like in the surf, when sand will work its way into the reel and play havoc with its mechanism—and in

A Battenkill Disc Reel. *Photo courtesy Orvis.*

the surf an expensive reel just isn't needed.) For the money, you'll find that the Battenkill 8/9 and 10/11 are the best value in quality saltwater fly reels available anywhere. They incorporate important features like disc drags, counter-weighted spools, anodized parts, and bronze bushings that are found on reels costing twice as much. These no-nonsense reels have served me well on a variety of inshore species ranging from corbina on Baja beaches to blues and stripers on Martha's Vineyard.

And then of course there are the renowned D-XRs. These moderately priced reels are the workhorses in the Orvis saltwater lineup and will handle just about every saltwater situation imaginable. I have used them on everything from bonefish to sailfish and they have always lived up to my expectations. Especially impressive is the drag mechanism. You don't need a drag system with the kind of stopping power you find on the lever-drag units featured on some of the big-game conventional reels; but the fly reel's drag must function flawlessly because with the lighter

An Orvis D-XR Fly Reel. *Photo courtesy Orvis.*

leaders used in fly fishing, there is less room for error. The drag must be absolutely smooth and remain so after long, repeated runs. The idea is to provide consistent, controlled resistance. If the drag jerks, you're going to lose most of your fish.

In this respect, the most grueling set of conditions I've ever imposed on my fly reels was a seven-day long-range bluewater trip where yellowfin tuna were the principal quarry. I used a pair of direct-drive D-XR Tarpon reels and they never let me down. A year later I am fishing the same reels and they have yet to require any repair work.

But the big news for those of us on the Advisory staff is the introduction of what we think is the finest saltwater reel ever made, Orvis's new Odyssey Series. Although the Advisory Team did a lot of testing on its own, most of the credit has to go to Orvis's engineering genius, Jim Lepage. After thoroughly analyzing every custom big-game fly reel currently available, Jim went right back to the drawing board. He even designed and built a $20,000 reel-testing machine, the only one of its kind. In a matter of hours it will tax a reel under conditions that would be difficult to duplicate in a lifetime of fishing. But laboratory tests are one thing; how a reel actually performs out on the water is another—and this is where input from the Advisory staff fishing the reel in every saltwater environment imaginable culminated in what we feel is the ultimate statement of the reel-maker's art. The Odyssey frames, feet, and spools are machined from aerospace-grade 6262 aluminum with a tough anodized finish that will ward off the ravages of saltwater. All the other parts are stainless steel. It is also the only reel of its kind to feature a unique engagement clutch that enables the drag to take hold the instant a fish makes its run. If there is even the slightest spool movement before a drag engages, the resulting sudden jerk is often all it takes to break the class tippet. The Odyssey completely eliminates this problem. From its unique design to its huge two-inch-diameter cork/composite drag surface, there is no reel like it on the market.

FLIES

DECEPTION IS THE KEY to all fishing with an artificial. You are trying to fool the fish into thinking that your unreal offering represents something worthwhile to eat. It's always a thrill when you can successfully pull this off, and there is an added measure of satisfaction when you get a fish to strike a fly that you have tied yourself. I'm not an artistic tyer and don't pretend to be. In fact, I'm always a bit reluctant to show people I don't know very well any of my flies. I don't think they look good—and many could be characterized as downright "funky." But at least one

FLIES RECOMMENDED BY THE ORVIS SALTWATER ADVISORY TEAM

A. Curcione's Tuna Tonic

B. Huff Backcountry Fly

C. Ruoff's Barracuda Fly

D. Ruoff's Backcountry Popper

E. Tabory's Snake Fly

E. Tabory's Snake Fly

F. Tabory's Slab Fly

G. Steve Huff Tarpon Fly

G. Steve Huff Tarpon Fly

G. Steve Huff Tarpon Fly

G. Steve Huff Tarpon Fly

H. Curcione's Sardina

I. Ruoff's Backcountry Bonefish Fly

J. Curcione's Big Game Fly

K. Ruoff's Lay-up Tarpon Fly

A big tarpon breeches. *Photo by Pierre Affre.*

Surf action. *Photo by Al Quattrochi.*

Leaping sailfish. *Photo by Nick Curcione.*

A great billfish leaps. *Photo by Linda Rogers.*

Surf flies for perch and corbina. *Photo by Cameron Ridell.*

Bonito flies. *Photo by Nick Curcione.*

friend has called a particular homemade popper of mine "fishy"—and that's what I'm after: flies that catch fish.

Years ago I made one of the early long-range trips out of San Diego. To my knowledge this was the first time that anyone ever brought fly-fishing tackle on one of these trips. It was early afternoon and we were hoping to top off a good day of wahoo fishing with a tuna bite at Soccoro Island. To stay out of everyone's way and give myself casting room, I would go up to the bow when other passengers were fishing the stern. I studied my "fishy" popper a few moments while the boat was being positioned and had to admit that no one would mistake it for one that came out of some fancy fly-fishing store. The finish was about as smooth as the boat's non-skid deck and the painted eyes were so misshapen that the thing looked like it was suffering from a terrible hangover.

In partial defense of this homemade creation I told myself that it was designed to catch fish, not the admiration of fellow anglers. And with a little help in the form of live anchovies as chum, it did just that. I tossed it into the midst of a school of yellowfin tuna that would periodically shatter the surface as they picked off zig-zagging baits with missile-like precision. On the first pass, in its effort to annihilate this strange creature struggling across the surface, a football-sized tuna plain missed it. But on the second cast a tuna with slightly better timing nailed it perfectly and I was onto my first fly-rod yellowfin.

If you have been fishing any length of time I'm sure you're well aware that so many of the artificials on the market are intended to lure fishermen as well as fish. What we sometimes forget, of course, is that what looks good to us may not necessarily appear so to the fish. All the advances in optics notwithstanding, we still know comparatively little about what fish actually see. With the exception of sharks, most of the laboratory studies in this area have not focused on open-water pelagic species. You can't put the likes of tuna, wahoo, or billfish in a tank and run controlled experiments on their visual patterns. Instead, most of what we know in this area has been accumulated from years of on-water trial-and-error experience.

What all this boils down to is that your saltwater flies do not have to come off as artistic masterpieces. Instead, what you should strive for is a reasonably good imitation of your quarry's principal food source. For example, on many offshore grounds the world over, the food source is primarily baitfish like anchovies, mackerel, sardines, and squid. Most of these baitfish have dark-green or blue-black backs and silvery sides and bellies. You cannot go wrong if you tie your flies to simulate these color patterns.

Regardless of what your creation may look like to human eyes, there are really only three relevant considerations: the fly's *fish appeal* (included here would be the fly's sink rate), its *castability*, and its *durability*.

The fly's fish-attracting appeal is actually a function of its color, size, silhouette, and sink rate. As stated above, if you tie most of your offshore patterns so that they incorporate the dark-green or blue-black backs and silvery sides and underbellies that predominate on most pelagic baitfish, you won't be far off the mark. We know that fish are taken on wild color combinations that can rival the creations of some avant-garde artists, but as a rule of thumb I think it's best to go with flies in colors that resemble what the fish normally eats. If that doesn't produce then you can always try something wilder.

Color is not as critical for surface poppers. Instead, the fish are attracted primarily by the surface disturbance. In these circumstances, color may chiefly be more a factor in helping the angler to monitor the popper. The popper I was using in the incident related above was yellow with a white underbelly. Since it rides on the surface, its underside is probably what the fish sees first so I painted it accordingly.

Another consideration when tying or selecting flies to imitate baitfish is the fact that most small creatures in the food chain have comparatively large eyes. They live in an environment where the unaware are quickly eaten so to help them survive they have evolved a good set of peepers. Eyes on a popper may not be too important because fish probably don't have a chance to key on them, but they should be an integral part of most streamer patterns.

The sink rate is a critical factor with streamers. You can be fishing exactly the same body of water with the same fly and experience radically different results depending upon the fly's sink rate. For example, bonefish do most of their feeding by foraging for crabs and shrimp off the bottom. If you want to draw strikes, this is where you have to get the fly. Sometimes, though, they will feed on tidbits suspended in the water column. So rather than have the fly drag bottom, you'll draw more strikes if your offering is suspended a foot or so above the sand. To accommodate these different requirements, the flies will have to be tied differently. In the first case, the flies should be weighted to facilitate their sink rate; adding a pair of bead-chain or lead eyes could be just the right touch.

Silhouette is the shape the fly takes in the water. Aside from simulating the body configuration of the fish's food source, as a general guideline bulkier flies tend to be more effective under conditions of reduced visibility, such as when fishing at night or in murky water. Just outside the breaker line off the beach, where the water is still a bit roiled due to the turbulence of the surf, I've had some of my best success on halibut using heavily dressed patterns that I originally tied for tarpon in the coffee-colored rivers of Costa Rica. By way of contrast, in the much clearer water offshore, sparsely dressed streamers will elicit more attention from members of the tuna family.

A popper's effectiveness in attracting fish is primarily a function of how it is shaped. If the object is to create a lot of surface commotion, then the face should be flat to offer maximum resistance and displace a large volume of water as it is pulled forward. In contrast, a bullet-shaped head creates a sliding effect without too much surface disturbance and is effective in quiet or protected waters where fish may be spooked by too much noise. Regardless of its shape, the hook should be glued only slightly into the underside of the body not midway through it. There must be a sufficient gap for the hook to penetrate effectively and hold.

The fly's silhouette, the amount and kind of material it's tied with, and whether or not it is weighted all affect its castability. Obviously, a small, sleek unweighted streamer will cast far more easily than something that resembles a feather duster. Poppers of course do not cast as well as streamers. Their bulky shape creates more wind resistance. This means that it will take more time for them to straighten out on the backcast. To adjust for this, you'll have to slow down your casting stroke a bit.

I don't know of any fly fishermen who wouldn't gladly sacrifice a fly in the interests of catching a fish. So when we speak of a fly's durability it is a relative matter. The offering, be it a popper or streamer, may not hold up too well after being mauled by a predator gamefish bent on consuming it, but it should at least withstand repeated use and continuous casting. If the air is shattered with material as you make your cast, the fly isn't tied properly. To make sure everything stays together I apply head cement whenever possible at each stage of the tying process. Applying a fast-drying epoxy to the final wraps of thread will add significantly to the fly's longevity. Epoxy also creates a nice smooth finish.

The heart of the fly is the hook and no matter how attractive the pattern, it doesn't mean much if you can't stick a fish. Two favorites of mine have been the Eagle Claw 254ss and the Mustad 3407. Bob Johns in Ventura, California, has been importing an excellent stainless-steel hook from Partridge of England. It has a straight-tapered loop eye that helps you make a neat job of tying off the heads on streamer flies. The Tiemco 800S is also an excellent hook for some saltwater flies.

All of your fly-tying hooks should be sharpened, preferably before you begin to tie on any material. Two very good files for this are a Nicholson Mill Bastard and the Hook File by Luhr Jensen. The best way to proceed is to secure the hook in a fly-tying vise. Insert the hook upside down so that the point and barb are fully exposed. Lay the file at a 45-degree angle along the outside center of the shank and take a few strokes in one direction, working from the point back toward the bend. Repeat the operation on the other side. You can take this a step further and form a diamond-shaped point with four cutting edges by taking similar strokes along the undersides of the barb. The point to this (pun intended!) is not to file away too much metal; otherwise the point will curl or simply break off. The way to test the hook's sharpness is to drag it across your thumbnail. If it digs in, it's sharp. A dull hook, and that includes most new ones taken directly from the box, will slide across your nail without sticking.

For those of you who are not fly tiers or just don't have the time, Orvis offers a great selection of saltwater patterns including a number of specialty flies designed by members of the Advisory Team. The latter will be referred to in the sections dealing with particular fisheries in Chapters 4 and 5, but for quick reference, consult the chart below.

Bonefish
Ruoff's Backcountry Bonefish: These flies feature deer-hair heads and
    lead eyes. In sizes 4 and 6.

Tarpon
Steve Huff's Tarpon Flies: In sizes 2/0, 3/0, and 4/0.
Ruoff's Lay-Up Tarpon Fly: In sizes 1/0 and 2/0.

Permit and Bonefish Flies. *Top row:* Del Brown's Permit Fly. *Bottom row:* (first two, left) Ruoff's Backcountry Bonefish Flies; (third and fourth from left) MOE, Bonefish Fly; (four on right) Bead Eye Charlie. *Photo courtesy Orvis.*

Snook, Seatrout, Redfish, Cobia, Jacks, Baby Tarpon, and Sharks

Huff Backcountry Fly: This unique pattern has a deer-hair head and rabbit tail. In size 1.

Ruoff's Backcountry Popper: In size 1.

Barracuda

Ruoff's Barracuda Fly: In size 1.

Stripers and Bluefish

Tabory's Snake Fly: In black or white, size 1.

Tabory's Slab Fly: Features a deer-hair head and glass eyes. In sizes 2/0 and 4/0.

Albacore, Bonito, Dorado, Skipjack, Yellowfin, Calico Bass, Pacific Barracuda, Cabrilla, and Pargo

Curcione's Sardina: In size 2/0.

Curcione's Tuna Tonic: A fast-sinking fly. In size 2/0.

Billfish, Large Tuna, Dorado, and Sharks

Curcione's Big-Game Fly: Tandem hook arrangement.

2

Fly Casting

THE INTERNATIONAL GAME FISH ASSOCIATION, the official record-keeping body for all facets of sport fishing, is quite clear in its definition of fly casting. In its regulations pertaining to fly fishing, the IGFA states that "casting and retrieving must be carried out in accordance with normal customs and generally accepted practices." Without getting into any semantic disputes over the foregoing, I'd like to point out that the IGFA's casting guidelines are not always strictly followed.

For example, when chumming for sharks in deep water the voracious critters often come right alongside the boat, and all you have to do to draw a strike is drop the fly in the water. I've also witnessed instances down in the jungle waterways of Costa Rica when anglers who weren't proficient casters simply flipped their flies over the side and let them play out sixty or seventy feet in the strong river current. These anglers weren't interested in records. They just wanted to catch a tarpon on fly-fishing gear and this was the only way they could.

From the standpoint of qualifying for a record, trolling is a no-no. In fact, the IGFA rules state explicitly that a boat's engine must be taken out of gear prior to making the cast. As much as I love to cast, however, I have to confess that I sometimes drag a fly behind the boat. I do this to locate schools of fish. Admittedly, this is a last resort, but if it puts me into fish I don't feel guilty about doing it. One action-filled day on Long Island Sound, after hours of successfully chasing bluefish that were mopping up frantic pods of menhaden that they had driven to the surface, the bite suddenly shut off. The blues had sounded, and it was time to shift from angler to hunter. But instead of merely confining ourselves to monitoring the fish-finding electronics, I dragged a fast-sinking line behind the boat. Before there was any indication of fish on the video screen, a bluefish intercepted my fly, and in a matter of seconds my other two companions were also into fish. The same tactic has worked many times out on the West Coast to track down schools of bonito and skipjack.

This isn't a case against casting. On the contrary, the foregoing are all exceptions to the rule that if you want to fly fish seriously, particularly in saltwater, you will have to learn to cast. Sadly, however, too often casting is the one dimension of the sport in which many fly fishermen are deficient. Over the years, in the course of countless trips and fishing clinics, I've encountered many anglers who were masterly fly tyers or who had a good working knowledge of knots and leaders, but who were less than adequate when it came to casting.

Fortunately, this is easily remedied. There is nothing mystical about fly casting and it doesn't require superstar talent. With good instruction, practice, and some plain old perseverance, just about anyone with average coordination can learn to cast efficiently.

HOW IMPORTANT IS DISTANCE?

LIKE MANY OF MY students who ask how long their term papers have to be, novice fly rodders frequently ask how far they should be able to cast. Part of the answer is similar to what I tell my students: there are no precise limits. When you are composing a paper you write until you have covered the topic. Likewise, you must cast a length of line sufficient to put a fly within reach of the fish.

The standard wisdom goes something like, "most fish take a fly that's only fifty or sixty feet away from the angler." I don't know of any records that have been compiled on the subject, but let's say that this statement is valid. But the reason for this belief has nothing to do with the feeding patterns of fish or their propensity to strike. Instead, it is simply due to the fact that many anglers are not able to cast effectively beyond those distances.

Remember that fish will sometimes follow a fly a considerable distance before striking. This occurs even with members of the tuna family, which are generally known for lightning-quick strikes when they spot an offering. Many times, while fishing for them on top with a splasher rig (this is described in Chapter 4), I've had several fish make repeated passes at the trailing fly for distances of twenty feet or more before one of them finally grabbed it. I have had similar experiences with bonefish. I remember a fish on the flats off Andros Island that followed my fly more than thirty feet before pouncing on it. I would strip the fly a few inches, and, like a cat stalking a mouse, the bonefish would wiggle its tail and follow without striking. This went on for what seemed like an eternity, until I was bent over like a washerwoman and my back and knees began to ache. Finally, with the tippet close to the tip-top, the finicky "ghost of the flats" decided that it would allow the fly to go no farther. In both these situations, if a long cast wasn't made initially the fish would not have had the opportunity to see the fly, pursue it, and eventually eat it.

Then, of course, there are times when you can't get into fish if you can't make the long cast, a fact of which I was reminded on a bonefish expedition to Christmas Island. For the first two days, a group of us fished flats on which the water was fairly deep. I stand six feet tall, and most of the time I was in knee-deep and sometimes waist-deep water. The bones were very cooperative and we didn't have to throw the fly more than fifty feet to enjoy great action. A few of the guests were relative newcomers to fly fishing, and after a couple of days of relatively easy angling they began to feel that their casting skills were more than adequate. Their smugness faded when we started fishing very shallow flats. We spent the better part of one day in water that was little more than ankle-deep, and their catch rate dropped significantly. The bones were extremely wary in this "skinny" water and often spooked if we waded within sixty feet of them. The anglers who were mediocre casters found that they couldn't reach the fish. But those who could throw a line eighty to ninety feet really enjoyed themselves. There's a good deal of satisfaction in enticing s skittish fish via a long-distance presentation.

We also fished for trevally, and they almost always required good casting technique. These are very strong fish, and if you are serious about pursuing them you should use at least a 10-weight outfit. Poppers yield the best results, but casting one of these large, wind-resistant offerings the necessary distance takes good technique. One fellow missed a great chance at a blue trevally in the 40-pound class that was cruising the edge of a coral flat about seventy feet from where we were wading. The fish was moving away from us and there was time for only one cast.

Unfortunately, the popper fell about twenty feet short, and before the angler could lift it from the water to make another cast the fish was out of range. This was unfortunate, because even at a remote location such as Christmas Island you may not get many shots at such a magnificent fish. It's always sad to see someone who has spent time and money on a long trip deprive himself of an opportunity to make a truly memorable catch simply because he never learned to cast properly.

And then there's the wind. No matter where you fish in saltwater, you will inevitably have to reckon with wind. It may not be a problem if you can cast with the wind at your back, but nature isn't always so kind. When you cast directly into the wind you may have to make the equivalent of a hundred-foot cast just to get the fly out sixty to seventy feet. So even if you don't always need great distance, it's important to be able to cast a reasonably long line.

BASIC FLY CASTING

JUST LIKE ANY SPORT that involves physical activity, you have to do more than merely read about fly casting; you have to go out and do it. To save time and minimize frustration, I strongly recommend that you team up with a good caster, preferably someone who is also a competent instructor. I have known very few people who were able to teach themselves to cast. And even in these cases, each angler had to spend a lot of time later to unlearn the faulty techniques he had acquired. Most folks today seem to have precious little time for leisure pursuits, so the last thing you want to do is go out and practice your mistakes. Just as you'd benefit by taking lessons from a golf or tennis pro, you'll be way ahead of the game if you get some top-notch instruction like that offered in an Orvis fly fishing school.

I was very fortunate in this respect because I learned from two of the best, Lou Tabory and the master himself, Lefty Kreh. Lou honed his casting technique under Lefty's guidance, so it's no coincidence that what I'm about to describe is known as the Kreh style of casting. There are other ways to go about it, but this style was developed by a fisherman for fishermen. When you master it, you will find that it will serve you well anywhere, whether you're fishing on a farm-pond-calm bonefish flat, in the pounding surf off a spot like Martha's Vineyard, or from the pitching deck of a sportfisherman plying the Pacific.

Watching a good fly caster is enjoyable in its own right. Even people who know little about the sport are often impressed by the graceful patterns of line flowing through the air. Everything seems so effortless and indeed, if executed properly, the process involves very little physical exertion. But to get to this point you have to learn to blend a series of steps into one smooth, graceful motion. All the steps are interrelated, so it's important that each in its turn be executed correctly. Faulty technique at one stage adversely affects what follows, and will diminish the overall effectiveness of the cast.

Whether or not it will be your principal outfit, for novice saltwater casters I recommend an 8-weight outfit with a weight-forward floating line. Most people find this easiest to work with at first. It's also best to begin on a calm body of water, such as a specially designed casting pond. If nothing like this is available, a wide-open grassy field is a practical alternative. You need an obstruction-free area because, with the exception of the roll cast, fly casting involves tossing the line behind as well as in front of you. Casting with conventional and spinning outfits also involves making a back cast, but with either of these you never have more than two or three feet of line behind you. In fly casting, however, thirty feet (or more) of fly line is thrown on the back cast. And, much like executing a proper golf swing, you have to make an effective back cast before you can make a good forward cast.

Beginning the Cast

You may recall or may even have been instructed in the so-called text-book method of casting, whereby a beginner was taught to cast with a book tucked between his body and casting arm. This was supposed to make for very controlled arm movements, but for most folks it felt awkward. In contrast, the technique I recommend is more comfortable because it feels more natural. The hips and shoulders come into play and there is extensive arm movement, which results in a far more fluid motion that makes the cast virtually effortless.

Grasp the rod firmly—but not too tightly—with your thumb on top of the grip. Rods with full-wells grips are the most comfortable to cast with because your thumb fits naturally in the indentation at the top end of the grip (this design is standard on all Orvis saltwater rods). Be sure your thumb remains in this position throughout the entire cast; if you turn it outward, you will alter the path of the rod and line, and the fly won't land where your want it to.

Begin the back cast with the rod tip pointed low, about a foot from the surface. The position of the rod at this very first step has a significant effect on your ability to lift the line off the water in preparation for the back cast. Even if you are casting from an elevated position, such as a rock jetty or breakwater, start the cast with tip held low. This seems simple enough, but most beginning casters fail to do it; they may start with a low rod tip, but by the time they actually begin picking line off the water for the back cast, the rod tip has crept upward several feet. In my experience, this is the most common fault among novice casters, but it is also the easiest to correct. Just remember to keep the tip low and don't raise it *at all* until you begin to lift the line from the water.

The point is to begin the cast without any slack in the line. The principle here is very elementary, and one day, while giving a casting lesson on a playing field near my home, the local fire department provided a great opportunity to illustrate it. The firefighters were going through a number of drills in which they practiced running out lengths of hose to connect to dummy hydrants. Each hose was wound in neat coils until a firefighter picked up the connecting end and raced toward a hydrant. The nozzle end never moved until all of the coils had been removed. Once the hose was completely straight, pulling on the connector end produced simultaneous movement on the nozzle end. The same principle applies to fly casting: before you can get the fly to move, all the slack in the line must be removed.

Let's apply this to casting. If you begin the back cast with the rod tip several feet above the water, you have created slack that has to be taken up before the terminal end of the line ever begins moving. This slack is removed by moving the rod up and back. Because the rod is already elevated, however, you have to move it that much farther to get a tight line. And putting a strain on the rod, which causes it to bend (this is referred to as "loading" the rod), can only be effected when the line is tight.

You want to use the rod's full potential to assist you in making the cast. When you have twenty or thirty feet of line lying in front of you on the water, it has to be lifted from the surface and thrown behind you. With the rod tip low to the water, strip in a little line until it is relatively tight. Now, with practically all the slack removed, you can begin to take the line off the water by raising your rod hand in a fairly swift, smooth motion. Try not to bend your wrist at the beginning of the lift. As you make the cast, the hand holding the line must not allow the line to slip; this will create slack, which always works against you.

The object is to lift as much line as possible from the water prior to making the "speed-up-and-stop" for the back cast. Continue raising the rod until it reaches just about eye level. Because your hand is positioned at the butt end of the rod, the tip will come up much faster than the butt. This will allow you to lift a great deal of line off the water.

Many people were (and still are) taught to cast by moving the rod in reference to the numbers on a clock. Briefly accelerating and immediately stopping the rod on the back cast (referred to as the "power stroke") was supposed to take place when the rod tip was at the one-o'clock position. This is fine, but you don't have to orient the casting stroke by telling time with the rod. Instead, the important principle is to make a very brief speed-up-and-stop motion, which doesn't necessarily have to be made at one particular location in reference to the clock.

For example, to extend more line on the back cast in preparation for shooting a lot of line on the forward cast, you will have to extend the distance you draw the rod rearward. This simply means that the speed-up-and-stop motion is made when the rod is back past your shoulder. And once that motion is made, do not allow the rod to drift back any farther, because doing so will cause the line flying out behind you to sag. Speed-up-and-stop means just that—at the point where the rod is finally stopped (and this may be way behind your shoulder), do not extend it any farther. Over-stroking at this point will create a wide loop in the line. This results in a very poor backcast, which in turn ruins your ability to make a good forward cast. For years, I was taught that a wide loop is inefficient because it's wind-resistant, but this really has nothing to do with it. A fat loop results when the energy imparted to the rod during the speed-up-and-stop action is dispersed over a wide area. Line speed is greatly reduced and the line flails out in a ballooning arc that seems to go nowhere. Failing to stop the rod, and to keep it stopped, will have the same effect on the forward cast and you'll achieve very little distance. To avoid this it's important to confine the speed-up-and-stop action to as narrow an arc as possible. This gives you a tight loop, which in turn directs the line in a nice tight flight path so it will lay out straight.

When you observe a good caster, this brief speed-up-and-stop action is effected so quickly that it's barely detectable, but it's there. It's in marked contrast to the wide, buggy-whip motion that causes a whooshing sound as the line flails past the caster who continues to apply power during most to the back cast.

After you have lifted most of the line off the water and made the speed-up-and-stop, the rod will momentarily have a nice deep bend in it. That is, it will be "fully loaded," much like a compressed spring ready to release stored energy. If no more power is applied, a properly designed rod will immediately stabilize, with no slack-inducing vibrations.

The Forward Cast

If you have done everything right up to this point, the line will fly out behind you in a nice tight loop. Just before the back cast has completely unfolded, begin coming forward with the rod hand. Experience will help you develop a feel as to the precise moment you should do this. But if you are just learning, there is nothing wrong with turning your head to watch the back cast. I usually have beginners do this so they can see what kind of back casts they are making.

Coming forward with the rod hand before the back cast has straightened out is contrary to the advice of some instructors, who will tell you to move the rod forward only after you have felt the line tugging behind you. But waiting this long is inefficient, because it lessens your ability to load the rod for the forward cast. By coming forward just before the line straightens out behind you, the tip section will encounter resistance from the line flying past in the opposite direction and you will get a nice deep bend in the rod with plenty of power for the forward cast. Moving your rod hand forward before the back cast unrolls completely also gives you a chance to smooth out any shock waves that may have developed in the line.

By moving your rod hand forward in a slightly upward, horizontal plane, the rod will continue to load. This is what effortless casting is all about: let the rod do most of the work for you.

The speed-up-and-stop stroke on the forward cast is essentially the same as that on the back cast. Just about at the point where your rod hand is passing your head, briefly accelerate and then stop the rod. Again, you don't want to exaggerate this; a very brief motion is all it takes. Even if you managed a tight loop on the back cast, if you over-stroke on the forward cast you'll end up with a fat loop. This is another common fault. When teaching beginners, I can often get them to make nice tight loops on the back cast, only to have their loops come apart on the forward cast. In part, this happens because a novice wants to put everything he has into the cast. Unfortunately, this usually accomplishes just the opposite. In contrast, if the rod has been properly loaded by moving it forward in an energy-gathering arc against the resistance of the line that's still flying backward, all you need is a quick burst of acceleration followed by an immediate stop to send the line out into the next zip code. As you stop the rod, move your line hand down and away from the rod butt. Do not drop the rod at this point. If you do, your loop will open and reduce the distance of your cast. Instead, slowly lower the rod as the line sails out overhead. Ideally, the rod should be lowered as the loop begins to unfold to maintain alignment with the line as it begins to fall.

BEYOND BASIC CASTING

IF THE FOREGOING STEPS are followed correctly you will be making excellent casts. But for added distance you will have to increase line speed, which is accomplished by means of the double haul. Bear in mind, however, that the double haul is no substitute for proper technique. So before you begin practicing hauls, master the basic steps.

Some people have been misled into thinking that they need the dexterity of a one-man band to properly execute the double haul, but that is pure nonsense. This technique is nothing more than two short tugs on the line made during the speed-up-and-stop strokes on the back cast and forward cast. Start the back cast with your line hand (the hand you will be making the haul with) a foot or so in front of your rod hand. Execute the normal lift-off of line from the water. When the rod is fully loaded, just at the point where you are going to apply the speed-up-and-stop, make a short, sharp downward tug on the line. You'll see some casters haul as if they were pulling on an outboard-motor starter cord, but that's not what you want to do. With a properly loaded rod this sort of exaggerated tug simply isn't necessary.

At the conclusion of the haul, maintain a tight line. Raise your line hand slightly, but not to the point where any slack develops; you want the line to feel taut. As the back cast unrolls, raise your line hand toward the rod butt. Make the next haul when the rod is fully loaded and has traveled forward to the point at which the speed-up-and-stop stroke is applied. The instant you accelerate the rod, haul sharply downward with the line hand. When combined with properly executed back and forward casts, the double haul results in very high line speed, and you'll be amazed at the distances you'll achieve.

The Speed Cast

Once you become fairly adept at the basics, there are two additional techniques that you'll want to add to your casting repertoire. One is the speed cast, a very important technique if you plan on fishing clear-water flats. This is fast-lane fishing in which things happen quickly, and to be successful you'll have to learn to respond accordingly. When they enter shallow water, even large species such as tarpon and sharks tend to be skittish. They move and change direction constantly, and you have to deliver your fly on a moment's notice—often within a span of 5 to 8 seconds. The speed cast is designed to help you do this.

Before you can make a speed cast, there are two preliminary steps that need attention. The first order of business is to make sure the fly line lays out nice and straight. Line that has been wound on a reel for any length of time can develop what is referred to as "memory": coils that need to be stretched out before the line will shoot smoothly through the rod guides. If you don't have anyone to help, you can do this yourself by grabbing a section of line and pulling your hands apart in opposite directions. If you are standing on an abrasion-free surface you can stretch your line by planting a foot on one end of a section while pulling up on the other end with your hand.

The second step involves rearranging the line so it lies properly for casting. When you pulled line from the reel, the heavy belly portion was the first to fall on deck. This was followed by the thinner running line. With the line reversed like this, the stage is set for a tangle when you attempt your first cast because the belly section has to work its way up through the rest of the line piled on top of it. What you want to do is realign the front and rear sections by making what I like to call a "sacrificial" practice cast. Then the line can be stripped in, with the heavier belly section coming in last so that it lies on top of the running line.

If the line fouls on a preliminary cast it's really no big deal. But when you're casting to a fish such a mishap can be disastrous.

The secret to making a speed cast is to start with as much of the belly of the line outside the rod tip as possible; twelve to fifteen feet is ideal. Since it is this heavy line that carries the thinner running line on the cast, it stands to reason that the more of it you have outside the rod when you start to cast, the faster you'll be able to load the rod and deliver your fly.

Once you have twelve to fifteen feet of line beyond the rod tip, grasp the tail end of the fly between the thumb and first finger of your line hand. This hand also holds a section of line picked up from the loose line lying on deck; use the last three fingers of your line hand to hold the line against the palm of your hand. When a fish is spotted, make a quick, sharp back cast, allowing the force of the line racing behind you to pluck the fly from your fingers. The slight resistance this creates helps to load the rod. Now make the forward cast. This is often all you'll need to get the fly to the fish. If greater distance is required, make a second back cast and shoot more line on the forward cast. At the most, it shouldn't take more than three back casts to get the fly on target.

It's important to maintain your grip on the line when the first back cast pulls the fly. On the final forward cast, let the line slip between your thumb and forefinger, but don't drop it. This way you are always in control of the line, and you'll have instant control of the fly. Even before the fly lands on the water, move your stripping hand over to the rod grip and trap the line under the first finger of your rod hand. This avoids the clumsy and time-consuming procedure of reaching for loose line before you can grab hold of it and bring it under the first finger of the rod hand. Wasted seconds can cost you a fish.

Casting Sinking Lines

You also need to learn to cast sinking lines. Unlike a floater, a sinking line cannot simply be lifted off the water, because it's under the surface, not on it. Before a backcast can be made, the line must be brought to the surface. The way to do this is by means of a roll cast.

Of course, if you have retrieved a sinking line until only a few feet of it remain in the water, you can start the next presentation by making a conventional back cast. However, if there are fifteen or more feet of line in the water, you will have to bring the line to the surface. Begin by slowly raising the rod tip; making a brief haul with your stripping hand will help get the line coming your way. Continue lifting the rod as the line slides along the surface, forming a deep bend as it glides toward you. When the line pauses in its path, make a sharp acceleration-and-stop forward and upwards. This stroke should be directed upward so the loop will climb and lift the line out of the water; as always, the speed-up-and-stop should be very brief to produce a tight loop. As the fly comes out of the water and the loop is rolling forward, start the back cast. Pulling the rod back at this point, with the loop still in the process of unfolding, will load the rod effectively. Now you can make a normal back cast, followed by the forward cast.

Regardless of the casting technique you use, you should be able to do it without undue exertion. If you feel like you just ran a marathon, you're working too hard. Rather than expending more effort, go back to the basics and practice good form. Hooking and fighting fish may be the name of the game, but once you become proficient, you'll find that making good casts is a pleasurable experience all its own.

3

Basic Fly-Fishing Techniques

STRIPPING AND STRIKING

A FLY IS RETRIEVED by pulling (stripping) line in by hand, and its movement in the water is directly governed by how you strip the line. How you handle the line also affects the manner in which you strike a fish. But fish, obviously, are not all alike, and different species display various mannerisms in the ways they approach and strike flies. To achieve consistent results you'll have to learn to accommodate different conditions. Regardless of the kind of action you want to impart to a fly, there are proper ways to strip line and it's very important to do it correctly. Let's look at two basic techniques. The first is the conventional one-handed method.

Hold the rod as if you were going to make a cast, with your thumb resting on the top of the grip. To control the line, cradle it under the first finger of your rod hand; bend this finger into a sort of U shape and the line will ride between it and the rod grip. Retrieve the fly by pulling in sections of line with your line hand. If you didn't have the line trapped under the rod, every time you completed a strip you would have to reach out and grab the line, which would have fallen away from you. As you can imagine, this would be very awkward and you wouldn't be able to strike many fish this way.

By manipulating the line by hand it's possible to impart an almost infinite variety of actions to a fly, something that is difficult to do by cranking a reel handle. Furthermore, with conventional and spinning tackle, lure action often has to be enhanced by moving the rod, and, depending on the rod's position, hook-setting effectiveness can be compromised. This is rarely a problem with fly-fishing gear, provided that the rod isn't moved while line is being retrieved. The principle is to always strike on a tight line, and this is difficult to do if you're waving the rod around as if it were an orchestra conductor's baton. If you start "jigging" the rod, slack is produced as the line jumps forward and forms a loose coil. You can't react quickly enough to gather in this slack if a fish strikes, and you probably won't achieve a positive hook-set because the line isn't under enough tension to drive the hook in.

Instead, keep the rod parallel to the water, with the tip pointed directly at the fly and the butt resting against your midsection. Should a fish strike, it will come up against firm resistance on a tight line. Tugging back on the line without using the rod will apply the most force to the fly, and will give you optimum hook penetration.

Some species of fish require a slightly modified technique. Billfish and tarpon fall into this category. A billfish is almost always teased to the boat, and you can see it take the fly. After the fish eats the fly, wait a second or two for it to turn with the fly in its mouth and then strike hard several times. It's best to cast the fly about five or six feet to the side of the fish; this way, it will have to turn to take the fly, increasing the chances of hooking it in the corner of its mouth. When you strike, use your stripping hand and rod hand simultaneously. Strip hard to the left with the line hand and pull to the right with the rod. This will exert maximum penetrating force. Essentially the same technique can be used for tarpon.

Two-Handed Stripping

The speed with which the fly moves through the water is obviously governed by how fast you strip in line. For certain species, such as wahoo, tuna and big barracuda, you just can't move the fly fast enough to interest them by using the conventional one-handed stripping method. To entice these high-speed predators into striking, you often have to make the fly streak through the water like a baitfish swimming for its life.

One way to create this effect is to sweep the rod to the right as far as possible (assuming that you're right handed) while simultaneously pulling on the line with your stripping hand. This will cause the fly to zip through the water for about ten feet or so. Unfortunately, that's the limitation of this technique; it's good for only a few feet. To make a fast retrieve over a considerable distance, use a two-handed stripping method. I recall one occasion in particular when the two-handed retrieve proved to be the hot ticket.

"Crank, man, he wants to eat it!" This was the simple-but-frantic piece of advice of skipper Frank LoPreste, as he tossed live anchovies to a wolf-pack of wahoo that was tearing into the terrified bait only a few yards off the stern of his super-sportfisherman, the *Royal Polaris.* The fellow next to me, who was on the receiving end of this directive, was retrieving a chrome jig in the hopes of enticing one of the ravenous critters to forego the real thing and chomp on his artificial. The instant the jig picked up speed, a wahoo that moments before had displayed only mild interest suddenly attacked the offering with such fury that a small roostertail was created by the line slicing through the water.

On this occasion speed was the name of the game, and those anglers who wanted to connect had to burn their lures through the water. Conventional reels with fast retrieve ratios of five or six to one are designed precisely for such conditions. But I was not equipped with a jig-casting outfit. Instead, to the amazement of my angling buddies, I positioned myself in the stern corner with fly-casting gear, deadly serious about nailing one of those speedsters on the long rod. My tackle may have been different, but the requirements for success were the same: I, too, was confronted with the problem of making an artificial lure move through the water as quickly as possible.

My Mylar-dressed streamer with all its flash looked great, but after repeated attempts I wasn't able to sucker a wahoo into grabbing it. If you have spent any time chasing these great gamefish, you know that they seldom remain in any one spot for long. So, despite the fact that we were fortunate enough to have them close to the boat eating our chum, I knew the action would be short-lived and this rare opportunity to score with a fly rod would soon be lost. In desperation, I changed tactics, and instead of stripping line in the conventional one-handed manner, I tucked the rod under my right armpit and began stripping line by alternately using both hands. This had the desired effect. The fly really picked up speed, and on my second try with the two-handed approach I was fast to my first fly-rod wahoo. From his higher vantage point on the bait tank, Frank saw the wahoo intercept the fly and his triumphant yell was at least as loud as my own. Within a few seconds the fish had streaked away with over a third of the thirty-pound-test Dacron backing. Needless to say, it was an exhilarating experience, but it would not have occurred had I not accelerated the fly's retrieve rate.

To achieve the same effect, some fly fishermen place the rod between their knees and then strip in line with both hands. From the standpoint of speeding up the retrieve rate, this is superior to the traditional one-handed stripping method, but it's an awkward placement and I recommended tucking the rod under your armpit instead.

Clearing and Controlling Your Line

"The moment of truth" is an expression that takes on various meanings in different sports. In fishing, it refers to the instant at which the fish takes the offering. This is especially true in saltwater fly fishing. Unlike most freshwater species, saltwater gamefish can create some potentially hazardous situations for the fly rodder. Ask any commercial fisherman who has ever heaved on a boat line with a wildly thrashing fish on the other end and you'll get a vivid picture of the kind of torture it's possible to subject your hands to. Anglers using conventional or spinning tackle generally do not have to be as concerned about getting hurt, but fly fishermen, because we handle the line directly, have to be extra-cautious regardless of stripping technique.

When a fish follows a fly before taking it, the line being retrieved will fall in loose coils on deck, in the stripping basket, or wherever you happen to be standing. Most saltwater gamefish go wild when they feel the hook, and the line laying at your feet will jump up and come whizzing through the rod guides like a compressed steel spring that's suddenly released. Your biggest concern at the point is to get the line under control and make sure it "clears" without fouling or tangling. Years ago, with one of my first fly-rod yellowfin tuna, I didn't react properly and the loose line leaped from the deck and knocked the long-brimmed cap off the fellow next to me, who had bent over to pull up a sock. Luckily, I still managed to clear my line.

With the one-handed stripping method, you control the outgoing line by forming a ring with the thumb and index finger of the line hand. Hold the rod high and have the butt end pressed against your forearm. If the reel is set up for left-hand retrieve, rotate your arm so that the handle faces away from the outgoing line. Allow the line to pass freely through the O you have formed in the stripping hand.

Follow the same procedure with the two-handed retrieve. Assuming that you are right handed, after striking the fish (and in many cases I feel this is done more effectively with both hands) form the O with your left hand, then grasp the rod with your right hand and move it out from under your armpit. It really doesn't matter if you have to grab the rod above the grip; the object is to first make certain all the loose line is cleared. Once your line has cleared, it's a simple matter to position the rod against your midsection and slide your hand down over the grip.

Advantages of the Two-Handed Retrieve

The two-handed stripping technique has a number of advantages besides making it possible to significantly speed up the retrieve. First of all, this technique enables you to more carefully control the fly's movement. By alternately using both hands to strip line, action is more easily imparted to the fly. Sudden starts, abrupt stops, barely perceptible twitches, and sudden sweeps are all highly facilitated when both hands come into play. With the traditional method, only one hand imparts action and even this is somewhat restricted because the line is being held against the rod by the index finger of the rod hand. By cradling the line in both hands, every hand movement is transmitted directly to the fly, enabling you to impart an almost infinite variety of gyrations. Some newcomers to saltwater fly rodding may underestimate its importance, but proper presentation of the fly can often be as critical as it is with the fussiest trout.

For example, fishing for permit on the flats might seem to have nothing in common with fishing for the popular corbina along a southern California beach, but the two species often display a marked similarity in feeding habits. Both are typically found in very shallow water, both spook at the slightest provocation, and both exhibit a frustrating tendency to be ultra-finicky in their willingness to accept artificials. In the case of corbina, the double-handed retrieve has proved invaluable in imparting the action that imitates a sand crab's movements and provokes these wary feeders into striking.

Because the two-handed stripping process is uninterrupted, you

have continuous contact with the fly. This will enable you to immediately detect the slightest resistance. Ed Mitchell, an avid fly fisherman from
Connecticut, prefers the hand-over-hand technique (as he refers to it)
when night-fishing for stripers with sand-eel imitations. A bass will often pick up the fly gingerly and continue to swim toward you. With the
conventional one-handed stripping technique, you might not even be
aware of the take, because the line is released by your stripping hand at
the end of each backward stroke before making the next strip. This brief
pause, during which the line isn't under tension, could cause you to miss
what's going on with the fly for a moment, and that's long enough to
miss a strike.

Finally, with the double-handed approach the line is not drawn
across your finger, and burns caused by abrasive line surfaces aren't really a problem. Today's line finishes are the best ever, but they often pick
up microscopic pieces of grit. In the process of constantly pulling line
across your index finger, a cutting action is generated, similar to the
effect of exposing your skin to a sander. Many fly rodders have had to resort to taping their fingers or even to wearing gloves. Stripping line with
both hands eliminates this problem. I still use the conventional method
in most circumstances, but there are times when two hands are better
than one, and two-handed stripping is a skill well worth mastering.

FISH-FIGHTING STRATEGIES

A REAL TEST OF both your tackle and fish-fighting skill is battling large
offshore gamefish from an anchored boat. For years, West-Coast anglers
embarking on multi-day trips (principally down off the Baja peninsula)
have pitted themselves against the likes of giant yellowfin tuna, challenging them without the benefits of a fighting chair or having the boat
follow the fish. The tackle may be different from standard tuna gear (although trips tailored especially for fly fishing are now being offered) but
the fish-fighting principles are the same.

Controlling the First Run

The process of subduing a gamefish can be broken down into three
stages. The first begins when the fish feels the hook. Depending on the
species and the situation, the fish may make either a very long run or
only a short dash to some type of structure. If you're in open water and

the fish is tearing off line you should try to exert enough pressure to coax it into stopping or turning before it takes all your backing. This is when following the fish with the boat is a great advantage; many outstanding catches with fly tackle would simply not otherwise be possible.

It's important to remember not to overrun the fish. If the boat moves too quickly the angler may not be able to maintain a tight line, and any time slack develops there is the danger that the fish can easily pop the line. You can demonstrate this principle to yourself by grasping a section of light line (four-pound-test, for example) in both hands and slowly pulling your hands apart. You'll see that even with small-diameter line it takes quite a bit of force to break it when it's being subjected to a steady strain. (In fact, to prevent cutting your hands you should wear gloves or wrap your hands with towels when performing this experiment.) Now take another piece of the same line, draw your hands together so a bow forms in the line, and snap your hands apart quickly. The line will break easily. This is exactly what can happen if you allow slack to develop while fighting a fish. If the fish decides to suddenly bolt, there's a very good chance that you'll hear a sickening snap, which tells you that the line has just broken and that you have parted company with the fish.

When a fish is running away and you can't chase it, you just have to hang on and hope that the drag pressure you are applying is sufficient to eventually stop the fish before you run out of line (this is known as getting "spooled"). Aside from considerations of sportsmanship, the possibility of losing all your line is one reason to use a tippet that is weaker than the breaking strength of the fly line. If your tippet is the weak link in the chain it will be the first thing to break, and you won't risk losing your fly line and backing.

When a fish runs for structure you can be faced with a genuine do-or-die situation. If the fish gets to where it's heading, chances are it will break you off. Your only alternative is to try to put the brakes on before the fish reaches the structure. The reel doesn't come into play right away because there isn't time to start winding line. Instead, you must apply steady, unrelenting pressure, and the most effective way to do this is by hand-stripping the line. Only when the fish is safely away from the structure should you begin winding in the accumulated loose line with the reel.

Drag pressure can be increased in a number of ways. The most obvious means is by tightening the reel's drag knob, but this generally isn't a good thing to do while actually fighting a fish because you can't react quickly enough to back off the drag setting if the fish lunges away or bolts. Remember, it's the sudden jolt that can snap your line. A better way to increase drag is to apply pressure with your fingers. There is no mechanical system that has as instantaneous a response time as the reaction time from your brain to your fingers. You can clamp the line tightly against the rod, palm the exposed spool rim, or push your fingers against the line on the spool. If the fish suddenly takes off, you can immediately reduce resistance by easing up with your fingers. Set your reel's drag lightly to begin with and apply additional pressure by hand. This is one of the secrets to landing big fish on light tackle.

As line begins to disappear from the spool, many anglers get overly anxious and try to stop a fish prematurely by applying more pressure. This should only be done as a last resort. In addition to drag produced by the bend in the rod, remember that as line is pulled from the reel, pressure on the fish is increased by the resistance of more line in the water. There is an increase in resistance as the radius of the line remaining on the spool gets smaller; it's harder to pull line from a half-empty spool than from a full reel. With 100 or more yards of line out, applying more drag on top of the steadily increasing resistance could easily break the tippet.

Fish that jump, such as tarpon or billfish, require special adjustments. Because a fish in the air is heavier than it is in the water, it can exert more pressure on the rod and direct more force against the fly that it's trying to shake loose from its jaw. To offset this, when a fish becomes airborne you must immediately reduce the strain on the line. This is most easily done by simply lowering the rod tip. The late Harry Kime demonstrated this to me many years ago when we were tarpon fishing in Costa Rica. The more common method is known as "bowing" to the fish; the rod is pushed toward the fish to create slack in the line.

Lowering the rod may sound contradictory to what I've said about maintaining a tight line, but the situation changes when a fish explodes into the air. Putting slack into your line creates a cushion effect. It's more difficult for an airborne fish to work the fly free on a loose line, and if it lands on line with a bow in it there is less chance of the line breaking than if it were taut. Harry's method of lowering the rod tip creates slack more quickly than does shoving the entire rod toward the fish. But whichever technique you use, always give acrobatic fish some slack.

Recovering Line

Once a fish has ended its run the second phase of the battle commences. This is when you must begin to work it back to the boat. An old truism states that when the angler rests so does the fish. To avoid needlessly prolonging the struggle, any time the fish takes a breather the angler must apply pressure to regain line. This is accomplished by "pumping" the fish.

Use the rod as a lever to help force the fish back to the boat. The object is to smoothly raise the rod from horizontal to vertical, until the butt is at approximately a 75-degree angle. When this point is reached, lower the rod and use the reel to take up line. Don't lift the rod so high that it's nearly perpendicular to the water; if you do, the pressure on the fish decreases dramatically. And by raising the rod too much the length of the downstroke is increased, and this can give the fish time to get its head down and use its powerful body muscles to dive. A much more effective technique is to "short-stroke" the fish. This means exactly what is says: a short lifting stroke—generally no more than a foot—is combined with a quick downstroke. You may wind in only a few inches of line at a time, but when you make short-strokes in rapid succession the fish usually begins to tire quickly and you can make it come your way in short order.

The Endgame

The third phase of the struggle is when the fish is close to the boat but not yet beaten to the point at which you have full control. This is a critical time, and many fish are needlessly lost because of mistakes that could easily have been avoided. The most common error is failing to back off when the fish makes a last-ditch bid for freedom, which it's likely to do just when you think you have it whipped.

When the fish is within fifteen yards or so of the boat, hold the rod low and at a right angle to the direction in which the fish is swimming. If the fish turns to the left, lay the rod over to the right and pull. When the fish turns to the right, lean on it from the left side. This keeps the fish off balance, and you'll be amazed at how quickly it saps its energy.

From the standpoint of conservation, beating a fish as quickly as possible is the proper course of action if you want to release it in prime condition. To a greater degree than many freshwater environments, saltwater is a truly Darwinian domain and large predators such as sharks are often lying in wait for an opportunity to seize a struggling fish. The longer a fish is fought, the greater the chances are that it will be eaten. Furthermore, a long drawn-out struggle can exhaust a fish to the point where it has little chance of making a full recovery. This seems especially true of very strong-pulling species like tuna. I have seen a number of these magnificent gamefish float to the surface dead because they simply exerted themselves to the point of no return. So while it's fun to use light gear, under some circumstances it may be not as sporting as heavier tackle, particularly if the battle is drawn out until the fish is harmed beyond the point of recovery.

4

Coastal Fly Fishing

SURF FISHING

WHEN YOU CONSIDER THAT a substantial portion of the U.S. population lives within easy driving distance of the Atlantic, Pacific, and Gulf coasts, and that long stretches of coastline remain readily accessible to the public, you can begin to appreciate the fishery that awaits the saltwater fly rodder. Ironically, in an age of crowded waters, most of this resource is under-utilized by fly fishermen.

At first glance, the coastal environment can seem downright hostile to fly fishing. The idea of chucking a fly into a pounding surf may seem about as sensible as riding a skateboard in an earthquake, and until you gain a little experience the elements can be intimidating. The surf does have its moments of tranquility, of course, but more often than not the breaking waves come ashore with a force that, over time, will pound jagged rocks into billiard-ball smoothness. Any time you wade an open beach you have to expect wind and churning water. Despite these rugged conditions, surf fishing has many redeeming qualities. Wading a stretch of snow-white surf on a nearly deserted beach can be every bit as rewarding as stalking trout in a tree-lined stream. And there are fish to be caught—tough, wily fish that offer great sport and a genuine challenge to the fly rodder.

The last thing I want to do is fuel arguments over what type of fly fishing is the most difficult or requires the most finesse. But I've heard some trout devotees disparage saltwater fishing based on the assumption that there is always some sort of wide-open action going on, in which virtually any offering is instantly attacked. True, there are wild feeding sprees the likes of which are seldom encountered on inland waterways. The plain fact, however, is that in most situations you have to work for your fish, and there are few settings as challenging in this respect as the surf. Regardless of the tackle, surf fish do not come easily; many of my friends who fish the beach with bait often come up empty-handed, and not because they lack talent. This doesn't mean that surf fishing with a fly rod is an exercise in willful stupidity. With persistence and know-how you will catch fish, and there are times when it is even possible to outscore those using bait.

Surf fishing can most definitely be classified as inshore fishing; as one veteran "sand jockey" expresses it, "Fishing the surf is as inshore as you can get." Many fish typically associated with bays, harbors, estuaries, and open stretches of coastline can also be taken right off the beach. For example, along much of the north and mid-Atlantic coasts, stripers, blues, and weakfish are among the species that shore-bound anglers can take on flies. When I lived back East I spent a great deal of time pursuing all three from a skiff, but two of the most memorable bluefish blitzes I ever experienced occurred while I was wading the Connecticut shore, once at Westport and a few years later off Stratford.

One of the factors that makes catching bluefish off the beach such an exciting prospect is that the action is often very visual and dramatic. Other species (striped bass, for example) can make their presence known by means of adrenaline-stimulating signs such as surface boils and diving birds, but few fish can match the top-water turbulence caused by blues on the feed. The surface churns like a giant jacuzzi, and there's something about being *in* the water that makes you feel part of the action. An added blessing is that you usually don't have to worry about boats roaring into the school and scattering your fish.

The overlap between surf and inshore species is perhaps nowhere as pronounced as on the beaches of the Sea of Cortez on the Baja Peninsula. Some of the favorite targets of angles fishing from skiffs (called *pangas* in Mexico), such as cabrilla, sierra, jack crevalle, ladyfish, needlefish, roosterfish, and even yellowtail, can also be found cruising the shore within reach of a reasonably proficient fly caster.

The species may differ radically, but the conditions you face on the east side of Baja are not unlike those you might encounter on a body of water like Long Island Sound. Both areas are characterized by a relative absence of pounding surf and churning water, which makes things easier for fly fishermen. More importantly, the signs indicating the presence of gamefish are essentially the same. Most of these signs will also help you to find fish in high surf and under a host of other inshore conditions.

Finding Fish in the Surf

The most telltale signs, of course, are the fish. Clear water often makes it possible to spot fish as they swim along the shore, but to do this effectively you should wear polarizing glasses. Even in places where the water tends to be off-color, polarizing glasses should always be on hand for daytime fishing; what little visibility there is will be greatly enhanced. In fact, any time you are fishing, some sort of protective eye gear should be worn. Orvis features some ophthalmic-quality glasses that are absolutely top-notch. They are offered in three different tints with non-prescription, single-prescription, or bifocal lenses. For most light conditions your best choice is a brown tint. In very bright light you should also wear a long-brimmed fishing hat, preferably one on which the underside of the brim is green.

Even with the proper glasses, however, you have to know how to look for fish. I'm always amazed by how well some guides who don't even wear glasses can spot fish. I remember one fellow in the Bahamas who simply shielded his eyes with his hand, yet he consistently spotted bonefish before I was aware of their presence. It wasn't that he had better eyesight—he just knew how to look.

If you are fishing in clear water less than three feet deep, the trick is to scan the bottom. Be alert for any movement that doesn't blend with the contours of the bottom. When standing on one of the piers in my home waters of southern California, this is how I search for corbina when they are prowling for sand crabs in close tight to the beach. I use the same technique walking along the shore when the corbina are in inch-deep water, but the surf makes it more difficult to see the fish; as each succeeding wave washes up, the water becomes clouded from sand that has been stirred up. But as soon as the water clears, studying the bottom usually reveals corbina working in and out of the wavelets looking for a meal. Stirred-up sand particles, which look like little underwater clouds, can also be an indication of corbina digging along the bottom. The same is true of bonefish probing for crabs and worms on a tropical flat.

In shallow water it's not uncommon to spot partially exposed tails and dorsal fins protruding form the surface. If the angle is just right, bright sunlight reflecting off a tail will look almost like a flashing mirror, and if you're alert it's possible to detect this far off in the distance.

Sometimes you may not be able to spot the fish itself, but its presence is evident from telltale movements in the water, such as a V-shaped wake on the surface. I caught one of my biggest trevally at Christmas Island after I spotted such a wake moving across the flat. I didn't know what was causing the wake, because the only thing visible was the parting water. I cast a popper about five feet in front of it and experienced the most explosive surface strike of my life.

In addition to V-shaped wakes, fish swimming near the surface can create a series of small ripples appropriately referred to as "nervous water," because that's just what it looks like. Any time you spot an out-of-the-ordinary movement on the surface, be on the lookout for fish.

Bird activity is another important clue to the presence of fish. This will be discussed in more detail in Chapter 5, but it's worth pointing out that regardless of where you fish, it's important to pay attention to the activity of sea birds, which very often feed on the same bait that gamefish do. When birds hover above an area it's a likely indication that they've spotted concentrations of bait and are in a holding pattern waiting for the bait to be driven to the surface by larger fish. Birds that are swooping down on the water are feeding. This doesn't always mean that there are fish in the area, but it's a good bet that when birds are able to pick baitfish off the surface, it's because larger fish are in hot pursuit.

You should also take note of bird activity on the beach. The best example that comes to mind involves sandpipers on southern California beaches. A major portion of the sandpiper's diet consists of sand crabs, which are also the favorite food of corbina and barred surfperch. Wherever you find these graceful, fleet-footed birds pecking away in the wet sand where the water laps the shore, you know that they're over a sand-crab bed. Chances are that the bed extends a few yards out into the surf, and if corbina or perch are your quarry this is where you should be fishing.

Understanding Tides and "Reading the Beach"

Good surf fishing can be had along practically all coastlines. But the key to consistent success with any species, whether it's striped bass in the Northeast or roosterfish off Baja, is learning to "read the beach," and you can't do this until you understand the tides.

Tides affect virtually all ocean fish, but their influence is especially strong on inshore and surf zone species. As most high-school students know, tides are created by the gravitational pulls of the sun and moon. The moon exerts the greater effect, two-and-a-half times that of the sun, because it is closer to the earth. But the sun's gravity also affects the tides. Twice a month, the moon and sun are aligned relative to the earth; in other words, a straight line could be drawn through the earth, the moon, and the sun. This alignment of gravitational forces gives rise to extremely high and low tides which are referred to as "spring tides." These occur during the full and new moons.

The opposite of this is the phase of lunar orbit when the sun and moon are pulling at right angles to each other, which results in a minimum rise and fall of the tides. These are called "neap tides," and they occur during the first- and third-quarter phases of the moon. A week of spring tides is followed by a week of neap tides, and so on throughout the year. What this means is that the tides change from week to week. If you had good fishing at a particular spot on a Saturday morning when the tide was incoming and high, by returning the same time the following Saturday you might well experience entirely different conditions and the fishing could be very poor.

Although surf species can be caught on all tides, there are some periods when you are much more likely to be successful. Tides cause water to move, and tidal currents have a lot to do with the fishes' food sources. An incoming or flood tide churns up the bottom, and on sandy beaches this stirs up food such as sand crabs and sand worms. In rocky areas, increased wave action can knock loose a variety of crustaceans. Fish are attuned to these conditions—they have to be if they are to survive. Like most creatures in the wild, fish do not have the luxury of setting their own feeding schedules. From birth, they are programmed to be opportunistic feeders, and when tidal currents stir the pot, inshore species set up feeding stations and start snapping up baitfish that are swept along with the tide.

Fishing is often best on an incoming tide, but it can also be productive on the outgoing tide. Churned-up bait is swept outward by a falling tide, and by getting your fly out a little deeper you can take advantage of this situation. During the slack periods, when there is little tidal movement, the best course of action is often to take a break and perhaps eat something yourself. But there are no absolutes in fishing, and there are some exceptions to the slow action normally associated with slack tides.

The behavior of fish in the surf zone is not unlike that of their freshwater counterparts, in that the physical makeup of their environment plays a major role in their feeding habits. To the untrained eye, most stretches of beach look pretty much alike, but this is not the case as far as the fish are concerned. Some sections will hold concentrations of fish while other areas are virtually barren. The trick, of course, is to fish potentially productive water.

In addition to having a working knowledge of tides, if you are going to ply the surf you must also know where to fish. Just as a trout

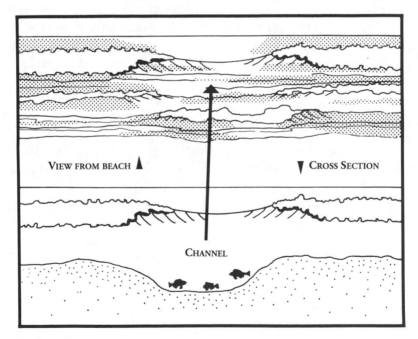

Beach-Surf View

fisherman learns to read a stream, you will have to learn to read the surf. This involves being able to observe the characteristics of waves as they roll in to shore and to then draw conclusions about bottom configuration from wave activity. The key is that waves *break* over shallow areas, while they tend to *roll* over deeper cuts or troughs in the bottom. If you observe a relatively flat spot on the water with waves breaking on either side of it, you've probably found deeper water above some sort of cut or bottom depression. Smaller sea creatures such as sand crabs, worms, and tiny baitfish that can't swim against strong tidal currents are swirled around and swept into the calmer water in these deeper spots. Larger predators are aware of this and position themselves accordingly. Water in these deeper pockets is less turbulent, and gamefish don't have to exert much energy to hold their positions. It's the same tactic that a trout employs when it holds behind a rock or undercut bank where there is a break in the current. The difference is that the water in a stream moves in only one direction; in the surf the current changes direction as the water rushes onto the beach and then recedes. This being the case, rocks on the bottom do not provide much relief from the current, and the fish have to find refuge in depressions in the bottom.

As waves roll toward shore they begin to break, and the troughs between the cresting waves are where you want to cast. This generally doesn't involve casting great distances. Many fishermen who use conventional or spinning gear often cast beyond the fish. The productive zone is seldom more than 100 feet off the beach, and even closer when you find a steeply sloping beach. A steep beach typically has deep troughs close to shore—sometimes not more than twenty feet away—and you want swim your fly in these cuts.

By marine standards, these bottom depressions aren't all that deep, seldom exceeding ten or twelve feet. Nevertheless, to get your fly down into productive water, a sinking line is a necessity. A fast-sinking line is preferable because you have a lot of turbulence to contend with, which can slow a fly's descent considerably. For years, I fished lead-core shooting heads almost exclusively because there weren't any commercial fly lines that could get my fly down quickly enough in this kind of water. Furthermore, the stiffness of a lead-core line makes it less prone to being buffeted about by the current; it tracks nice and straight on the retrieve. The actual weights (in grains) of lead-core lines aren't always indicated,

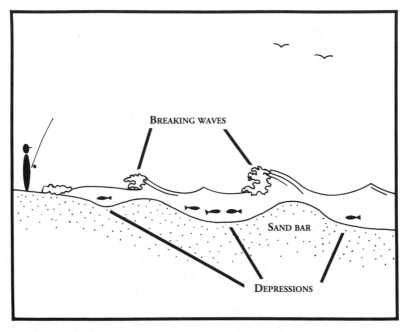

Beach Cross Section

so the best way to determine what length head balances with your rod is to go out and cast the line, gradually cutting it back in one-foot increments until you get the desired match-up. For example, on the 8-weight rods that I generally use for smaller surf species such as surfperch and corbina, I've found that heads from twenty-three to twenty-six feet long make for a balanced outfit. Lead-core lines have a couple of drawbacks: they tend to kink and those with plastic coatings usually do not hold up well under the abrasive effects of sand. The latter is not a problem with Orvis Lead-Cord Shooting Heads, and since their introduction I have used them extensively in the surf with good success.

Adding to the challenge of surf fishing is the fact that bottom contours can change almost daily, especially when stormy weather and pounding waves create new holes and depressions. An area that was productive one day may not be good the next. Therefore, it's best to work large stretches of beach in search of congregating fish. Once you get a strike or land a fish, it pays to work that area over thoroughly because it's probable that other fish are holding there. Over the course of hours of wading and casting, you may nail most of your fish within a span of minutes. Unlike bait fishermen, who will generally stick to one spot, a fly fisherman can sometimes be more successful by constantly moving and covering a lot of water.

How Habitat Influences Fish—and Your Fishing

"Reading the beach" involves more than just monitoring wave action. It also includes learning to recognize the importance of coastal features such as rock outcroppings, reefs, patches of sea grass, shoreline-hugging kelp and the composition of the bottom itself. All of these exert an influence on the ecological chain, which in turn determines the availability of the species you seek.

Freshwater bass fishermen may have been the first anglers to popularize what is now commonly known as "structure fishing," but the principles are essentially the same in salt water. Jetties, breakwaters, natural rock formations, submerged reefs, kelp forests, stone-studded beaches, and soft bottoms all provide habitats for a variety of marine organisms such as crabs, mussels, clam worms, barnacles, rock shrimp, sand eels, and many types of baitfish. These in turn attract an equally diverse lineup of inshore and surf-zone gamefish. In each case there is an interplay between habitat and the availability of a particular species.

For example, let's look at a baitfish chain that develops along some West Coast beaches. The different varieties of Pacific surfperch all bear their young live, and sometime between March and July the two-inch-long fry swim free of their mothers. This doesn't mean much if you're interested only in catching perch. But the spawning habits of surfperch become significant when your attention turns to other species such as halibut and calico bass, which invade the surf zone when the silvery tidbits are available. Grunion runs also bring larger fish in to the beach, and whenever they or surfperch fry are the primary food source, it's time to "match the hatch." The pattern that I've found most productive under these conditions is a white Lefty's Deceiver. When barred perch fry predominate, I use Deceivers from one-and-a-half to two-and-a-half inches long. Grunion are larger, generally from four to six inches long, so I tie flies with longer hackles to imitate them. Calico bass have bucket-size mouths, and patterns tied on size 3/0, 4/0, or 5/0 hooks work fine. For halibut, I like to go with size 1 or 2 hooks.

The largest halibut I've ever taken on fly was caught in the surf in Baja. I was perch fishing with friends who were using dead anchovies as bait. To keep the perch in a feeding mood, every so often my friends tossed out handfuls of "chovies" in the trough line. This provided fantastic action on the fly rod, and for the better part of forty-five minutes I hooked big, fat female perch on practically every cast. Then two of my friends hooked up with halibut, and I could see a free-swimming, pillow-case-size "flattie" skimming the trough, apparently gorging itself on the fry that were being released by the female perch. I quickly substituted a small Deceiver for my sand-crab pattern, and after a dozen or so casts the line came tight so abruptly that at first I thought I was hung on the bottom. But when the line began to slide through my fingers with a steady, determined pull, I knew that I had hooked the kind of halibut that had eluded me for years. About twenty minutes went by before I was able to surf the "door mat" onto the wet sand. It blended in so well that if it hadn't flopped a few times I would have had to follow my line to pinpoint its location on the beach. A beat-up old hand scale, which was about as reliable as a kid telling you how big his first fish was, put the halibut at the twelve-pound mark. It may have weighed less, but I still consider it one of my all-time best catches on the fly rod.

Calico bass are a prolific species, and you can expect to fare very well when they're in the surf. Grunion, perch fry, and an invasion of pelagic crabs can really trigger their feeding instincts. When the crabs hit the coast, instead of trying to tie exact imitations I find it easier and just as productive simply to duplicate their size and color—from about two to three-and-a-half inches long, with a reddish-orange tint. Dan Blanton's Whistler pattern, tied with splayed orange neck hackles and bucktail or FisHair, is very effective.

Much like striped-bass fishing in the Northeast, some prime spots for calicos are the rock ledges that punctuate the Southern California and Baja coasts. These ledges are home to a variety of species, and they attract larger predators that feed on the smaller baitfish which often congregate around them. Because some of these ledges jut out a good distances from shore, you can cover a lot more water than would be possible casting from the beach. These rocks can place you anywhere from ten to forty or more feet above the water. This height, coupled with the powerful backwash created by waves smashing against the rocks, means that a hefty rod is required to muscle the fish though the turbulence before it ends up snagged on the rocks. This is especially true with larger species such as striped bass. And when you fish from these ledges it's sometimes impossible to beach your catch as you can on a sandy shore. If the fish has any size to it, landing it may even require help from a partner.

This is when a heavy-duty rod really comes into its own. More beef in the butt section makes it possible to lift a fish so that it can be gaffed or tailed. There are places where it is either impossible or simply too dangerous to attempt climbing down to reach a fish, and in these circumstances a powerful rod such as a ten-weight HLS Keys Special or an eleven-weight Power Matrix-10 will make the job of maneuvering the fish to a more accessible spot a lot easier.

The rocky beaches and cliffs of the Pacific Northwest also offer some fine fishing for a species that many of the local anglers refer to as bass. Their body structure and predatory instincts resemble those of calico bass, but they are a different species. These rock-dwellers are members of the scorpion-fish family (Sebastes), more commonly known as rockfish. Much like calicos, the black rockfish and its close cousin the copper rockfish are structure-loving species. They are attracted not only to rocks, but to kelp or any man-made structure such as pilings or riprap that offers a combination of concealment, a respite from the strong turbulence of the surf, and, last but not least, the opportunity to establish a feeding station.

Like most surf species, rockfish are opportunistic feeders and will dine on a variety of food sources, including crustaceans, bloodworms, and small eels. Deceivers or leech patterns with tails and collars made with strips of rabbit fur are effective offerings. But because these fish prefer snag-infested bottoms, your flies should be tied bend-back style so the hook points ride up. Fish over four pounds are considered large, with average catches ranging between two and three pounds. Rockfish have large mouths, so you can tie flies on size 1/0 to 4/0 hooks. Low-light conditions—foggy or overcast days, dawn, and dusk—are when rockfish are most likely to go on the feed, and it is best to fish during slack-tide periods when there is minimum water movement.

In the Northeast, a very important baitfish for shore-bound fly fishermen is the sand eel. These are a favorite of bluefish and striped bass, and even bonito, which aren't typically associated with beach fishing, can be accessible targets when sand eels are abundant. But, like most marine organisms, you won't find sand eels on just any stretch of shoreline. Sand eels, as their name implies, like to bury themselves in the sand. This is not for spawning, as is the case with grunion, but apparently to avoid being eaten. Considering this ostrich-like defense posture, the most productive shorelines to fish are those with soft sand or mud bottoms. Since sand eels can't very well burrow into rock-strewn or hard bottoms, these are places to avoid. (Incidentally, sand eels are fish, not eels, their snakelike shape notwithstanding.)

This is also a situation in which you want to "match the hatch," at least in terms of size, silhouette, and color, and Lou Tabory's Sand Eel patterns are convincing imitations in all three respects. When I first saw a sand eel I remarked how closely it resembled the anchovy, one of the primary baitfish on the West Coast. After I returned to California, it was only logical to give Lou's flies a try, and, as testimony to their versatility, I've used them to catch bonito in the harbors and calico bass in the kelp beds.

Taking note of the bottom composition is also important when fishing for West Coast species such as corbina and barred surfperch. From the Santa Barbara area, south to mid-Baja, the latter are the surf species that will most readily take a fly. Compared to most saltwater gamefish, barred perch are small; most taken along California beaches weigh about a pound and a half and rarely exceed ten or eleven inches in length. They can go over four pounds, but a three-pounder is considered a real prize. In over twenty years of pursuing them my largest surfperch to date was a Frisbee-sized specimen that weighed two pounds, fourteen ounces. (It won a perch derby in which there were over 200 participants; I was the only one who used a fly rod.)

The best time of the year to fish for barred perch is from January through March, and in some years, right through April. In January, the larger females come into the surf from deeper water in preparation for their annual spawning ritual. They also come in search of food. The primary food of both corbina and perch are thumbnail-size crustaceans that burrow into the beach. Known locally as sand crabs, they are one of three species of mole crabs found along the Pacific Coast, and in their soft-shell molting state they are prime bait for corbina and barred perch.

Barred surfperch. *Photo by the author.*

Their presence in the sand is often indicated by V-shaped indentations. If you are barefoot you can sometimes feel them as they burrow into the sand. And, as mentioned earlier, keep an eye out for sandpipers, which also relish sand crabs.

An excellent pattern for perch and corbina is a simple fly I designed and named Beach Bug. Tied on a size 2 or 4 hook, its basic shape resembles a sand crab, and a bright orange chenille hump simulates roe on the underbelly of egg-laden females. I have also had good success with attractor patterns tied Comet-style in bright red, orange, and yellow. To my knowledge these do not resemble any food source, but perch, and to a limited extent corbina, apparently find them to their liking.

While perch fishing is most productive during winter and spring, corbina fishing is primarily a summer and early fall affair. July and August, when large populations of sand crabs congregate along the beach, can be peak months. More than any other surf-zone species, corbina bear a close resemblance to bonefish. Their body configurations are roughly similar and they both feed extensively on essentially the same class of sand-dwelling organisms. And when they're probing the bottom for a meal, both have a penchant for very skinny water. Corbina may not

Corbina. *Photo by the author.*

spook quite as readily as bonefish, but they are much more difficult to entice with artificials. Even fishermen who use live sand crabs often experience difficulty drawing strikes.

Sight-casting to corbina that are searching sandbars in just inches of water is closely akin to stalking bonefish on a tidal flat. Early morning, right after sunrise, is usually the best time to do this. Most beaches are virtually deserted at daybreak and there is generally very little wind. This is also one of those times when fishing a slack tide can be best; there's not much water movement from breaking and receding waves, so instead of darting to and from shore the corbina tend to swim parallel to the beach, making them much easier to spot.

To avoid alerting the fish, under these conditions it's best to cast from the sand and not even enter the water. A slack tide also calls for a change in presentation strategy. Even though you may be fishing a stretch of beach exposed to the open ocean, the shallow water and relatively calm conditions dictate a specialty line, and the Orvis Clear-Tip is the best I've found for conditions like these. The ten-foot intermediate tip is clear, so it's less likely to put off wary fish in shallow water. In line weights six through nine, which is the ideal range for corbina, the line has a long front taper that makes for delicate turnovers even with short leaders.

Regardless of the species you pursue, the experience of a throbbing fish battling you in the middle of a boiling surf is a sensational feeling. You are contending with the elements as well as the fish, and landing it under such conditions requires a little technique. The trick is to not become overly eager and try to muscle the fish onto the beach. It's easier and more effective to let the waves do some of the work for you. For example, if the fish is close to shore and the water begins receding (taking the fish with it), do not pull back, because the added strain can easily pop your tippet. The best course of action is to run to the water's edge to give line and reduce the strain. When the water begins to push shoreward you can put the pressure on and actually "surf" the fish onto the beach.

Auxiliary Gear for the Surf and Shallows

Fishing from shore, whether off a beach, a breakwater, or a rock ledge, poses some special challenges for the fly rodder, and there are certain items you do not want to be without. One of the most important is a stripping basket. If there is anything that can possibly catch or snag your line, you can bet that sooner or later it will. (That's why serious offshore fly fishermen take extra care to prepare the deck area from which they will cast.) The rough surfaces of jetty boulders won't do your line any good, and, more importantly, they can also tangle or foul your line when you cast. This is particularly true in the surf, where water turbulence will create endless tangles and snarls if you simply allow your line to fall into the water. Even under calm conditions I don't like to drop my line in the water, because the surface adhesion impairs my casting; even a floating line lying on top of the water doesn't pick up as easily as it would if it were lying on a flat, dry surface. The solution is to use some sort of container to hold the line as it's being retrieved after each cast. In fly-fishing parlance such a container is called a stripping basket.

I used to make my own stripping baskets from plastic dishpans because they worked better than anything that was available from fly-fishing specialty shops. Then Orvis introduced a stripping basket called the Tangle-Fee Shooting Basket, and it really lives up to its name. It's made of vacuum-molded polyethylene with nine tapered cones in the bottom to keep your line from tangling. A quick-release adjustable nylon belt is woven through four slots in the contoured back wall, which fits comfortably against your waist. I've used this basket in practically every situation imaginable, from the surf to Mexican pangas in which I could hardly stand the clutter, and it has worked perfectly every time. It's so handy that I never go on a fishing trip without it, even when I have to travel; it packs easily in soft luggage, and I pack clothing and gear inside it.

Whenever fishing involves wading, some type of protective foot gear is usually in order. About the only time I go barefoot is when I'm fishing for corbina during the summer, when most of my casts are made from dry sand. But the safest course is always to wear something on your feet. The new Orvis Superlight Tuber/Flats Boots are the most versatile footwear of their kind. They're very comfortable, they protect your feet from sharp rocks and coral, and the lace-up design means that you don't have to fuss with zippers that get fouled with sand or grit.

Regardless of your footwear, any time you wade a warm-water flat where there might be stingrays, walk by dragging each foot forward with your toes skimming the bottom. If there is a stingray partially buried in the sand this will alert it and it will swim off before you step on it. This happened to me once on the flats off Belize, and I was so startled when the ray sprang forward that I fell backwards in the water.

If you don't have the luxury of fishing in warm-water areas, you'll need insulation against the cold, and chest-high neoprene waders are the most practical choice. Even in my home waters off southern California, I wear them most of the time when surf fishing; this stretch of Pacific is cold. I've collected plenty of waders over the years—my garage looks like it's filled with the rejects from a rubber factory—but my favorites are Orvis Boot Foot Neoprene Waders. The fact that the boots are integral parts of the waders makes them easy to put on and take off. And for the first time, I can walk on the sand and not feel as if I'm dragging bowling balls.

Of course, any time you proceed on foot you'll need some means of carrying your flies, leader material, pliers, file and whatever else you might require. The Orvis Convertible Saltwater Pack makes carrying these items simple. It has three pockets inside, two pockets outside, a tippet dispenser in the outer flap, and it's constructed of Cordura with corrosion-resistant hardware.

Always wade carefully, no matter where you fish. Be especially cautious in the surf. A good practice is to try to stay in water that's about shin-deep. Wading any deeper can get you into trouble; the undertow can sweep you off your feet if you're not careful. Naturally you want to watch the waves, particularly so if you're perched on top of a rock ledge, jetty, or breakwater. Before venturing out into any of these, study the wave patterns for a few minutes. If some are breaking where you plan to fish, consider other options.

BAYS AND HARBORS

BACK IN THE EARLY 1980s, when I had a seat on the Pacific Fishery Management Council, I quickly learned that fish don't recognize political boundaries. They follow nature's script and go where they need to. Nor do they recognize the categories that anglers establish, and the distinction between inshore and offshore fishing tends to be somewhat arbitrary. There are a number of species, such as bluefin tuna, yellowtail, and some sharks that can be found both relatively close to the beach and far out to sea in the blue water. I have hooked yellowtail right off the beach in the Sea of Cortez, but I've also found them beneath floating kelp patties more than twenty miles from shore.

But one has to draw the line somewhere, so I'll leave the aforementioned species and a few other for the next chapter. For now, let's concentrate on some of the more popular species available in bays and harbors and in the open ocean within a few miles of the coast.

Ironically, my introduction to bay fishing with a fly rod took place with a friend who is a spinning enthusiast. He knew I loved to fly fish, and was the first person to encourage me to give it a try in Newport Bay, California. Admittedly, the very first time I was skeptical. I had been on the bay many times before, but not to fish; it had always been the point of departure when I was fortunate enough to be invited aboard a luxury sportfisherman bound for Catalina Island or some other offshore ground. I hadn't contemplated fishing where some of those very boats are moored.

On that first fly-fishing trip, Newport Bay looked like a scene from "Lifestyles of the Rich and Famous." It was certainly beautiful enough—the sunrise splashed an array of pastel hues on the yachts and multi-million-dollar houses that line the shore. I sort of got caught up in the splendor, and my friend must have known what I was thinking, because he assured me that we would soon get into fish. I realize now that my initial skepticism was simply due to the fact that I let the sights get the better of my fishing savvy. Some of the best-equipped fishing yachts on the West Coast were heading out of the harbor, and the bemused looks of the skippers, eyeballing the two of us in my little skiff from atop their tuna towers, made it seem like they were doing the right thing, not us. But as soon as I started to ignore the displays of wealth, I realized that we were in prime holding water for a variety of species. My hopes were confirmed when I got my first strike and my line went as tight as a telephone cable.

We were using an electric motor to hold us about fifty feet from one of the private boat docks while I cast my fly to within a foot of the pilings. Such structure is home to a variety of marine organisms, and the fish that feed around it don't have to move very far for a meal. If your offering isn't right on target, the fish are not likely to swim out to get it because they don't have to. The fly rod can be a decided advantage in such a situation, because once you have stripped out the right length of line you can make repeated presentations with pinpoint accuracy. I started at the end of the dock, and cast to each piling in succession, thoroughly covering every potential holding spot. At the third piling I got a strike. I made two short, sharp strips to set the hook, and felt a powerful tug that seemed way out of proportion to where we were fishing.

My friend anticipated my thoughts again when he laughed and said, "These are very strong fish for their size." When I hand-stripped the fish to the boat a minute or so later I knew what he meant. The fish was a spotted bay bass of about two pounds, but the ferocity of its strike and the tenacity with which it fought had led me to believe that it was considerably larger.

We accounted for over forty fish on that trip (I took seventeen on the fly rod), and on subsequent outings I found that our success wasn't just a chance occurrence. The action in the bay is frequently as good and sometimes even better than you might encounter offshore. True, the fish are smaller, but if you work the right tides (incoming and outgoing highs are best) they are usually quite cooperative and chances are you'll catch a mixed bag that includes halibut, barred sand and calico bass, spotted bay bass, yellowfin and spotfin croaker, corbina, and surfperch. You might even tie into striped bass (they have been introduced to Newport Bay), white sea bass, barracuda, or bonito.

There is great fishing to be had in the bays and harbors on all coasts. One of my most memorable encounters with tarpon was inside the Naval Air Station at Key West. A retired high-ranking officer made arrangements for a few friends and me to sample an evening's fishing inside the base. This may sound like a fish story—I didn't believe it until I saw it—but one of the Marines standing guard would occasionally get splashed by a tarpon picking shrimp off the sea wall. We hooked only two fish that night, but I was ready to enlist.

Protected backwaters such as Newport Bay and Key West Harbor (and numerous other bays and harbors) are biological horns of plenty. The water is relatively shallow, seldom exceeding forty feet in depth, and tends to be several degrees warmer than the outside sea water. This encourages the growth of marine plant life and a host of micro-organisms, and, coupled with the abundant nutrients washing in from the sea, makes for a rich ecosystem, while docks, piers, and moored boats provide cover for small baitfish and their prey. In short, there's a lot for gamefish to eat.

Fishing in sheltered waters has many advantages. Sea sickness is not a problem, and you don't need a large boat or the kind of accessory equipment that can put a dent in an oil sheik's bank account. Inshore trips are also fairly easy to arrange. Many bays and harbors are near major metropolitan areas, within easy reach of practically anyone who can drive a few miles. For fly fishermen, inshore waters are a resource which has barely been tapped.

POPULAR INSHORE SPECIES

AS WE'VE NOTED, MANY species available to anglers fishing from shore can be found—and caught—in the protected waters of bays and harbors. But fishing for stripers in the surf isn't exactly like casting to them in the middle of a calm bay. Each marine habitat presents its own opportunities and challenges, and can call for specialized skills and tactics. So can each species of fish. Although it's enormously helpful to study marine ecosystems, it's also essential to examine the behavior and feeding habits of particular types of fish. The coastal fly fisherman, after all, can pursue an astonishing variety of species. Let's look at those you're most likely to meet in inshore waters.

Striped Bass

It's doubtful that any species has drawn as much interest from saltwater fly fishermen as the striped bass. The striper's striking and fighting qualities make it a superb gamefish, and, with weights that can top the thirty- and even the forty-pound mark, it reaches very respectable proportions. Best of all, stripers are truly "people friendly" fish. Their proximity to major cities such as Boston, New York, Baltimore, Washington, D.C., and San Francisco puts them within reach of more anglers than any other saltwater gamefish.

During the last twenty years, there have been dramatic shifts in striper populations on both coasts. A few developments have been positive, while others, sadly, have been disappointing. When I returned to California in the early 1970s, I was fortunate enough to enjoy the tail end of what was once an abundant fishery based in the San Francisco Bay area. Unfortunately, water-diversion projects have caused a steady decline in the area's population of adult stripers. Millions of striped-bass eggs and fry have been pumped into the canals that make up the California Central Valley Project. This has been a terrific boon to freshwater striper fishing because the fish are thriving in inland impoundments such as the San Luis Reservoir, but it has depleted the San Francisco Bay Fishery. Meanwhile, on the East Coast, particularly in New England, conservation regulations and pollution-abatement projects have led to steady improvement in striped-bass fishing since the mid-seventies.

Like many other inshore gamefish, stripers are very opportunistic feeders, but unlike species that tend to be somewhat sedentary, such as fluke, halibut, and Pacific rockfish, stripers are nomadic when they're searching for food. They do, however, establish favorite foraging stations around particular kinds of structure, and near holes in the bottom and troughs that parallel sand bars. Such areas serve as havens for various types of bait, which in turn attract stripers and other gamefish. Particularly in the Northeast, some of these feeding stations are located in estuaries, on shallow flats, and right inside the surf line along beaches. These areas are tailor-made for wading. In fact, in many cases it would be neither practical nor prudent to use a boat. The only alternative is to wade, and this is not without its advantages. Aside from considerations of accessibility, stealth, and the pure fun of it, you will develop a heightened sense of awareness as you gain experience fishing on foot. Instead of relying on electronic aids like depth gauges and fish finders, the wading angler must learn to make full use of the senses nature provided him.

The sense of touch becomes especially important when wading for stripers. Bass often lie in the slower currents found in the bottom depressions that form just below rips. When you are in the water you can feel even subtle changes in current, which might very likely go unnoticed if you were in a boat. You also get a very accurate feel for the bottom, and the slightest changes in contour become immediately apparent. And when stalking stripers, knowledge of the bottom can often spell the differences between fruitless casting and catching fish. For example, stripers have a habit of lying in the deeper water that drops off the side of a sandbar. But to avoid alerting and spooking the fish, you should begin casting before you reach the high point of a bar. This may not be easy to determine from a boat, but when wading you'll feel the slight incline that tells you you're approaching the bar, and this is where you want to start casting.

Another very effective method of pursuing stripers on foot is jetty fishing. "Jetty jockey" is an Eastern term that originally referred to baitcasters and spinning enthusiasts who fished from this type of structure, but it has become an apt description of fly rodders, particularly those after stripers. In the Northeast there are many jetties that were built to protect beaches from erosion and prevent harbor and river mouths from becoming unnavigable. But as far as fishermen are concerned, their principal function is to provide havens for bait. Just as they do with natural structure, some types of bait, such as cunners and eels, take up residence inside jetties, while other creatures may seek only temporary refuge. Either way, larger predators are drawn to these spots to feed.

This is a situation in which a fly could very well prove to be the most effective offering. One of the major advantages of streamer patterns tied with saddle hackles, marabou, bucktail, or FisHair is their ability to "breathe" in the water, closely simulating the movements of baitfish. And unlike most lures, which are likely to snag on a jetty, streamers can be fished close to the crevices, rocks, and pilings where stripers are most likely to forage. Long casts aren't often necessary, particularly at night, when stripers can be feeding practically at your feet.

The most productive zones around a jetty are the rips that often form along the sides and end points. You also want to work the white water that rolls behind or alongside sandbars adjacent to the jetty. If you're on a jetty at the entrance to a river or harbor, an outgoing tide is usually best because it carries bait out from the sheltered water. Try to fish the down-current side whenever possible, because this is where bait will be pushed when the tide begins to flow.

Given the nature of the forces that drive bait close to a jetty, proceeding on foot is often the most efficient way to go. Whether bait intentionally seek this structure or are carried there by the current, the fact remains that a good deal of the time the prey is packed in tight to the rocks, and it's not always practical or safe to work such areas from a boat. In addition, bait often seeks sanctuary from predators along the jetty and will sometimes swim in toward the rocks, rather than away from them. Therefore, standing on the jetty and retrieving your fly back toward you simulates the movement of bait trying to avoid being eaten.

Fishing for stripers on foot does have its limitations, however, and sometimes a boat is necessary. Fortunately, you generally don't need something on the order of an offshore sportfisherman to fish safely. Conditions will vary, but since stripers are primarily a shoreline-hugging species, you can fish effectively from a small skiff in many places. But don't be lulled into a false sense of security because you're close to shore. Always be alert for changes in weather and sea conditions, and be especially cautious when fishing outside the surf line along open stretches of beach.

On the West Coast, small-boat striper fishermen working just outside the surf line find some of the best action in Central California along the rugged San Mateo shoreline from Thorton Beach to Lindamar Cove, and San Francisco Bay has long been a hot spot for skiff-fishing for stripers. In the Northeast (the birthplace of West Coast stripers), anglers are blessed with hundreds of miles of productive shoreline. Areas such as Buzzards Bay, Martha's Vineyard, and Nantucket Sound, the

Rhode Island coast, Montauk, and the south shore of Long Island Sound down into New Jersey consistently produce good striper fishing for private boaters. To the south, the Chesapeake Bay area offers excellent small-craft striper fishing.

For fly fishermen, working from a boat can be a decided advantage because it allows you to cast to spots that cannot be reached from shore. Lou Tabory, whose passion and forte is wading for stripers in the surf, recounts many frustrating experiences when he had to stand by and watch skiff fishermen battle bass that were busting bait just beyond his casting range.

A skiff also makes it possible to cover vast stretches of water; if one area fails to produce it's easy to move on to more promising spots. One of the most effective ways to look for fish is to drift over shallow flats.

As many anglers have learned, medium- to fast-sinking shooting lines are often ideal for such conditions. When you're wading, a slower-sinking intermediate line may be more practical because you are often working the fly from deep to shallow water. But drifting in a boat is very different from wading. When you cast at an angle to the direction of the drift, your line is likely to be pulled toward the surface as the boat moves. Even in water that's only five to eight feet deep, a fast-sinking line will help keep the fly in the productive zone. Some anglers shy away from these lines for fear of constantly hanging up on the bottom, but this generally isn't much of a problem. Even a moderately paced drift will help keep the line and fly from dragging bottom. Furthermore, stripers often seem to prefer a fairly quick retrieve in which the fly is stripped back in rapid two-foot pulls of line, and with such a retrieve there is less chance of the fly settling on the bottom and becoming snagged. And there is always the option of using a fly tied bend-back style so the hook point rides up.

In keeping with the striper's diverse diet, there are a variety of fly patterns that consistently take fish. Besides sand-eel imitations, there are Tabory's Snake Fly and Slab Fly, Dan Blanton's Whistler series, Ed Givens' Barred-and-White and Barred-and-Black, Clouser Minnows, Janssen's Striper Fly, the Bay-Delta Eelet, Lefty's Deceivers, and the Whitlock Sculpin. The size of your fly can be more important than the pattern. If you get repeated refusals, you may want to change to a longer

Lou Tabory's Bluefish/Striped Bass Fly Selection. *Clockwise, from top:* Tabory Slab Fly, Tabory Snake Flies (white, black, and white), White Tabory Slab Fly, Popper or Skipping Bug, two Deceiver patterns *(at 7:00)*, another Tabory Slab Fly, a Popper or Skipping Bug, Sand Eel *(at 10:00)*. *Photo courtesy Orvis.*

or shorter fly before switching patterns. Most striper flies are tied on hooks from size 1/0 through 5/0, and you should always carry different sizes of each pattern.

Your rod (or rods) should be matched to the conditions you expect to confront. For casting to pilings, rip rap, and other structure, rods in the ten- to twelve-weight class may be the way to go. This is tug-of-war fishing, and you really have to apply pressure to turn a fish and get it coming your way. Like any fish that's close to structure, the striper's first instinct is to head for protective cover. This may only be a lone piling, but if the fish succeeds in getting around it, your line or leader can easily be severed. The largest striper I ever hooked parted company with me when it turned around a bridge support. The strike was especially aggressive even by striper standards, and when the bass turned I caught a glimpse of its broom-size tail when it broke the surface. I applied all the pressure I could with the eleven-weight rod I was using, but I couldn't stop the fish from dragging the leader across the bridge support.

This is a contingency you have to be ready to deal with when fishing around structure. Striped bass are tough and aggressive, and with those over the ten-pound mark you'll find that sometimes no matter how much pressure you apply they will manage to cut you off. You can often draw vicious strikes by casting under a dock or pier, or between the pilings and supports of a bridge. In these situations, at least in the initial stage of a battle, I don't even think about trying to use the reel. The prime objective at this point is to try to turn the fish your way; otherwise there's a good chance it will head into the structure and you will never even see it. If there is loose line lying on deck, rather than taking time to wind it on the reel it's more effective to pressure the fish with the rod and hand-strip line until the fish is safely away from the structure.

On open-water flats, nine- to eleven-weight rods will generally provide all the pulling and lifting power you need. And with today's advanced graphite materials, these rods are not only effective fish-fighting tools, they are also a pleasure to cast. There are occasions when you may spot breaking fish, but much of the time you'll have to blind-cast to cover as much water as possible. This is when you really appreciate a rod that isn't going to wear you out during hours and hours of casting. My personal favorite for conditions like these is the nine-weight Power Matrix-10; without a doubt, it is one of the best-casting nine-weights I've ever fished.

On shallow flats most of the striper action will be subsurface, but when they're busting bait on top you'll want to have a weight-forward floating line for casting poppers. Captain Pete Kriewald would definitely agree: he has the distinction of catching one of the largest stripers ever taken on a popper, a forty-five-pound brute he nailed back in 1973 at Goose Island off Norwalk, Connecticut.

Bluefish

Slammers, choppers, Long Island piranha, or just plain blues—regardless of the local name, there's no question that bluefish are one of the most exciting inshore species. The only negative comment I can make

Fish will often feed extremely close to a jetty, as the flurry of baitfish at Martha's Vineyard shows. *Photo by Lou Tabory.*

about them is that they aren't found on the West Coast; bluefish are the one species I miss most since returning to California.

It's hard to think of a coastal species that has more to offer. Like striped bass, bluefish are within fairly easy reach of many major metropolitan areas. Nantucket, Martha's Vineyard, the entire coast of Rhode Island, Montauk, New Jersey, and Chesapeake Bay are all prime spots for bluefish from late spring right into late fall. In fact, they can be found all along the East Coast.

Another very attractive characteristic of bluefish is that they never seem to have lockjaw. Like jack crevalle, they're nearly always ready to feed. And if there were a category for wild antics, the bluefish would take top honors. I have witnessed some awesome feeding sprees by members of the tuna family, but in terms of all-out frenzied action I've never seen anything that can match a bluefish blitz. If the sights and sounds of explosive surface swirls, screaming birds, and terrified pods of baitfish don't push your emotional circuits close to overload, you should probably consult a neurosurgeon. When you hook one the reaction can be as violent as putting spurs to a bucking bronco.

The most exciting scenario is when they invade the shallows. From Maine to as far south as the Carolinas, migrating blues start roaming the skinny water as inshore temperatures begin to rise into the 60s. You may dream of taking trips to exotic locales, but it's difficult to find better sport than casting to blues that can top the ten-pound mark in water that may be less than six feet deep.

A 9-weight outfit is generally perfect for shallow-water blues. The fish can't sound, so you don't need a rod with a great deal of lifting power. A weight-forward floating line should be your first choice for blues in the shallows, but you might also want to have a sink-tip on hand. Heavy surf or deep water, particularly when you're after larger bluefish, call for beefier 10- to 12-weight outfits. Blues sometimes feed on top in deeper water, but you'll need a fast-sinking line for most deep-water fishing.

As some of their nicknames imply, bluefish have formidable teeth. When you consider that a bluefish also has jaws that can clamp shut like a machine-shop vise, you can see why shock leaders are very important. For clear water, where blues can become a little leader-shy, there are some anglers who recommend a mono shock leader instead of wire, but there is really no advantage in using mono. First of all, you would have to use fairly heavy mono—at least 60-pound-test. But if the blues are spooky, such heavy line might put them off as quickly as wire. And experienced anglers will tell you that in many cases even 60-pound mono doesn't hold up against a bluefish's teeth; you might just as well take your chances and forego using a shock leader altogether (but I would try this only with a popper or streamer tied on a long-shank hook, and I'd hope that the hook's extra length would be enough to keep the line from those scalpel-sharp teeth). In general, however, the safest course is to use wire. The trick here is to keep it short—no more than four inches; otherwise your fly won't turn over properly. Orvis Super-Flex Shock Wire is very handy because it knots more easily than standard wire. But with any wire, it's best to use the smallest diameter possible. For blues, Super-Flex in 24- or 32-pound-test is adequate.

Because bluefish are such aggressive feeders, your flies can be basic and simple: poppers and standard streamers like the Lefty's Deceiver are usually all you need. Poppers can be tied on hook sizes from 1/0 to 4/0, and yellow or white are two popular colors. Deceivers can be tied in all-yellow, white, and blue-and-white on hooks from size 1 to 2/0. One of the few occasions when it might be necessary to "match the hatch" is when blues are feeding on one particular type of baitfish, such as sand eels. Depending on the size of the bait, patterns for sand eels can be tied on hooks from size 4 to 1/0. Lou Tabory, originator of one of the classic sand-eel patterns, likes to tie his with green-over-white bucktail and several strips of 1/64-inch silver mylar. He has also had consistent success with white-and-yellow, all-yellow, and all-black patterns.

Weakfish and Spotted Seatrout

Weakfish, or squeteague as they're known in New England, have a special meaning for me. In June of 1973, just before returning to the West Coast, I participated in a weekend conclave sponsored by the Salty Fly Rodders of New York. I was a member of the Connecticut Saltwater Fly Rodders, and, thanks to a yellow streamer tied by John Posh and a massive dose of plain old blind luck, I caught the largest weakfish of the trip. The commemorative plaque still hangs in my home.

I remember the great weakfish runs in Peconic Bay when I was a youngster. It wasn't uncommon for savvy fishermen to take literally bushel-basketfuls of fish. Most of the weakfish in those days weighed between two and three pounds, but occasionally heavyweights that topped the ten-pound mark would move in and temporarily grab the spotlight from stripers and blues.

Along the Eastern Seaboard the weakfish's range roughly parallels that of striped bass. They seldom venture into the cold waters north of Cape Cod, but you can find them from Martha's Vineyard to North Carolina. They have a varied diet much like that of stripers, but, being smaller, they show a preference for scaled-down versions of sand eels, crabs, sea worms, and such. In the creeks small shrimp are a favorite food. The scope of their diet accounts for the fact that weakfish can be taken on a variety of flies, ranging from a small half-inch Shelter Island Weakfish Fly to Lou Tabory's five- and six-inch Sand Eels. The most

At fading light, inshore fish often start to feed vigorously. At Shelter Island, New York, two anglers hook weakfish. *Photo by Lou Tabory.*

consistent action, however, is with smaller streamer patterns, and yellow is the most reliable color.

I'm not exactly sure how weakfish got their name. Perhaps it has something to do with the fact that their fighting prowess is not up to striper or bluefish standards. It might also be related to the "glass jaw" syndrome that plagues some boxers. These fish have a delicate section at each corner of their mouths, and if you're not careful your hook can easily tear out. Therefore, it's not good practice to strike back very hard with your stripping hand. Likewise, it's best not to apply maximum pressure. Although weakfish have teeth, they generally do not pose much of a problem and a shock leader isn't really necessary.

Areas such as the shallows of Long Island Sound and Delaware Bay can be heavily congested with boat traffic during peak summer months, but by nightfall these same spots are practically deserted. During the springtime, small creeks and outlets throughout the Northeast can provide outstanding weakfish action, and for those who like to ply the shallows after sunset, nighttime can be the best time for tossing flies to weakfish. They feed in essentially the same manner as stripers, holding in one spot waiting to ambush bait as it is flushed along in the current. This is when you want to bring along a floating line for casting surface poppers and darters. Tabory's Floating Shrimp Fly will also draw strikes and is particularly effective in small creeks.

Spotted seatrout bear a close resemblance to weakfish, but they run slightly larger and prefer more temperate zones. Some get as far north as New York, but they are most abundant from the mid-Atlantic shores south to Florida. They also provide good fishing along the Gulf Coast.

Whereas weakfish will suspend over different types of bottom, seatrout favor shallow bays with plenty of grass. Drifting across these flats and using basically the same technique you would use for stripers is a very effective strategy for taking seatrout. It's important to swim your fly through the grass beds and close to the bottom, so a fast-sinking line is in order. Slow to moderately paced retrieves seem to draw the most strikes, and bend-back flies let you fish in the grass without getting snagged. Unlike weakfish, seatrout don't respond well at night, at least not to flies, so this fishery is primarily a daytime affair. They will also take surface poppers, but, as with weakfish, the most consistent action will be right off the bottom.

THE BIG THREE OF THE FLATS: BONEFISH, TARPON, AND PERMIT

FOR MOST AVID SALTWATER fly fishermen, working a shallow flat in water as clear as a freshly cleaned window pane is close to angling heaven, perhaps because more is demanded of the angler than in any other form of the sport. In many respects, flats fishing represents the ultimate challenge in fly fishing in the salt. The quarry must be spotted, often under conditions that can deceive and impair one's sight. Once detected, the fish usually requires a careful, unobtrusive approach. Your cast must often be fast and accurate, and your fly has to land as softly as a wind-blown feather. And once hooked, the fish runs wildly because it cannot dive for cover; it can only streak across the bottom or leap into the air. In either case, your tackle and fish-fighting technique will be tested to their limits. But equaling these demands is the tremendous sense of satisfaction you feel when you've put it all together and met the challenge.

Of course, bonefish, tarpon, and permit are not the only gamefish available to fly fishermen on the tropical flats. Barracuda, jack crevalle, redfish, sharks, snappers, and snook are also found in the same waters, and all will respond to flies. And you might have a chance encounter with a black drum, cobia, or tripletail.

In northern climates, bluefish and stripers will stalk the shallows, but the "big three" are strictly warmwater species. Bonefish and permit prefer water temperatures between 70 and 85 degrees Fahrenheit. Tarpon usually won't show unless the water temperature is above 75 degrees.

Just as in surf fishing, understanding the importance of tidal fluctuations is absolutely critical when fishing the flats. When you're fishing in areas where depth is measured in inches, not fathoms, the effects of tidal movement are dramatically obvious even to the untrained eye. In the early morning you might be in knee-deep water; by late afternoon, the same flat could be bone dry, devoid not only of fish but water as well.

Even with basic knowledge of tides, observing and applying their effects on the flats takes considerable experience, and it's best to have a local guide, at least to get you started. Every area has its own peculiarities—one flat may be best on an incoming high tide while another is more productive when the tide is ebbing.

The volume and strength of the tidal surge will also determine when fish will swim onto and leave a flat. On a spring tide, for example, when the high tides are higher than average and the low tides lower, fish will tend to arrive earlier on an incoming tide. By the same token, because there is a greater volume of water emptying the flat on the outgoing phase, they will also depart earlier. Furthermore, the volume of water can affect where the fish will be; in high-water conditions fish will sometimes move farther up on a flat. If it's lined with mangroves they may take cover under the branches, considerably reducing their accessibility.

Bonefish and other predators on the flats behave differently under varying tidal conditions. When water is spilling off a flat faster than normal on an outgoing spring tide, the fish may become more skittish. Conversely, when there is more water than usual covering a flat, the fish may be a bit less wary. There are, of course, trade-offs. In water that's only about a foot deep there's a greater likelihood of spotting tailing fish, but they'll probably be very nervous. When the water level starts approaching the three-foot mark, the fish lose some of their caution, but visibility is significantly reduced and you'll have a more difficult time picking out a target.

With the exception of a few noisy offerings such as poppers, we rely mainly on the fish's sense of sight to detect our flies. Much more than many anglers realize, however, fish also rely a great deal on smell to help locate food. If we adhere to IGFA fly-fishing guidelines, we are not permitted to enhance the appeal of our flies by dousing them with any of the scents commonly used by conventional and spin fishermen. All we can do is present our flies in the same places (relative to the fish) as the bait that fish are initially attracted to principally by aroma. Here again, knowledge of tidal actions is a key ingredient to successfully fishing the flats. As a general rule, species such as bonefish, permit, and redfish tend to swim headfirst into the tidal flow. I guess for the fish it's somewhat akin to standing downwind from an Italian delicatessen. The tidal current carries the scent of a variety of food sources and nature has programmed predators to position themselves to intercept these aromatic messages. As a case in point, it's estimated that under ideal tidal and wind conditions bonefish can detect the scent of shrimp, crabs, or conch as far as 100 yards away.

A great way to take advantage of this is to chum. Begin by selecting a flat known to hold bonefish. Because you will be sight-casting to the fish, try to pick an area that has a light-colored bottom or a patch of white sand. This provides a contrasting background that makes it easier to spot fish as they move in to pick up the chum. Guides in the Bahamas often use pieces of conch, but in Florida the chum usually consists of shrimp diced into half-inch sections. When a guide has a new client, one of the first things he wants to determine is the client's casting ability. Before staking the boat in position, the guide will have the angler cast to see how much line he or she can handle effectively. The boat will then be secured at a spot from which the angler can comfortably cast to the chum. Ideally, the sun should be at one's back, and of course the boat has to be up-current from the chum. If bonefish are in the area, they will inevitably home in on the scent. Since stronger tidal currents carry more bait and its accompanying scent, the most opportune time to fish the flats is often during spring tides, when there is maximum tidal flow. This chumming technique isn't limited to bonefish, of course.

Bonefish

They may lack the size and dramatic airborne antics of tarpon, but thanks to their legendary wariness and speed, bonefish continue to draw legions of anglers who rank the "ghost of the flats" as their number-one gamefish. Practically every species manages to attract a following, but the passion and devotion engendered by bonefish are unique. There are saltwater aficionados with vast experience in practically all phases of the sport who still regard stalking bonefish on a flat as their favorite pastime. And when freshwater fly fishermen decide to expand their sport to salt water, the species that most often marks this transition is the bonefish. Fishing thrills, like beauty, may be in the eye of the beholder, but I haven't met anyone whose emotions aren't stoked by the sight of bonefish tails slicing the surface like translucent wafers. Even non-anglers are stirred by the sight of bonefish. I remember a couple from Austria who made a trip to Christmas Island primarily to view the bird life. One afternoon I invited them to wade a flat with me where I knew there would be a good chance of spotting tailing bones. I don't understand German, but I recall having to motion to them to be quiet so I could get off a cast. The lady was flapping her arms like a teenager standing before a TV camera. With all the commotion the fish moved off, but the couple soon understood the necessity of a stealthy approach and I was able to hook a fish from the next pod we encountered. In a chivalrous move I handed the lady the rod and, after a number of frantic bilingual exchanges, she landed her first bonefish. The fish had barely been revived and released when they began asking if it was possible to rent fly-fishing gear on the island. (As at most resorts, the answer was no, and for that reason alone you should always bring along at least one backup outfit. On more than one occasion an unfortunate angler has had his gear lost somewhere, and having a spare outfit to lend him could save an otherwise disastrous outing.)

Bonefish are more widespread than tarpon or permit. They are caught in Hawaii and as far out in the South Pacific as Christmas Island, which is the latest "mecca" for bones. The Caribbean (the Bahamas and Turneffe Flats), Mexico (Ascension Bay), Cuba, and Central America (the flats off Los Roques) are all well-known areas. Some have even been reported in the backwaters of Newport Bay in Southern California, but in all the years I've fished there I have never seen one.

An angler wading a Caribbean bonefish flat. *Photo by Lefty Kreh.*

If you do want to fish for bonefish in the continental U.S., Florida is the place to go. In fact, unlike fishing for some other "glamour" species, there are a number of places in the Keys where you don't even need a boat to reach them. All you have to do is park your car and literally wade right in. Starting at Key Largo, Card Sound Road will take you to the northern part of the island, giving you access to the flats on the ocean side which remain some of the most productive and least-fished areas in the Upper Keys. From Key Largo south all the way to Sugarloaf Key, there are a number of good flats on the ocean side of the Overseas Highway. Long Key, Grassy Key, Ohio Key, Big Pine Key, and Summerland Key all offer quality bonefishing. For those who prefer to fish from a skiff and remain close to a metropolitan setting, there is Biscayne Bay, where you can catch bonefish against the backdrop of Miami's skyline. Specialized skiff fishing predominates, however, particularly in the lower Keys, where many of the top flats guides base their services.

The bonefish population in the Keys remains fairly abundant throughout the year, but they are a tropical species and strong cold fronts will drive them off the flats. At the other end of the continuum, they generally do not tolerate water temperatures above 88 degrees. With this in mind, you should adjust your fishing times to take into account variations in seasonal temperatures. For example, like many anglers who visit South Florida, my vacation time is concentrated during July and August. This is the hottest time of the year and the skinny water on the flats can heat up like a child's wading pool. Under these conditions you'll have better fishing during early-morning and late-afternoon tides, when the water is cooler. Just the opposite applies during the winter months, when midday fishing is often best because the water has had a chance to warm up a bit.

As for the best bonefishing tidal stage, most experts would pick the first two or three hours of an incoming tide. But given all the variables—wind, prevailing temperatures, the type of flat, its location, and where you happen to be—the most accurate statement is that there is no single best tide. The optimum times depend on a host of local conditions, and simply trying to locate fish on a consistent basis is one of the principal challenges in bonefishing. To reiterate, the services of a local guide are invaluable.

The size of bonefish is apparently related to the area where you choose to fish for them. Some of the biggest bones are found in Biscayne Bay, where they average about eight pounds. Bill Barnes, who fished this area for years before he took up residence at his Costa Rican lodge, Casa Mar, took sort of a busman's holiday a few seasons back and put me on a bonefish that looked like it could have gone over ten pounds. They say the larger ones get that way because they're smarter and this one proved true to form by refusing my fly. By way of contrast, at Christmas Island you'll see a lot more fish but they tend to be smaller, in the three- to five-pound range. But irrespective of locale, the smaller fish tend to travel in schools or at least groups of three or more fish, while the big boys are usually loners. And, of course, it's the single fish that requires a more careful approach; when a bonefish is alone, it's more wary. Also, since there is no competition from other fish, a lone fish seems less inclined to strike a fly. Like most species, larger bonefish are more difficult to catch.

The standard fly line for bonefishing is a weight-forward floater. By incorporating feedback from its endorsed-guide program, Orvis has come up with a Tropic Fly Line designed especially for fishing in very warm water. A new formulation keeps it from becoming limp and sticky, and it will shoot through the guides easily even after lying on a hot deck. Tropic Fly Lines in weights 6 through 9 have longer front tapers that make for delicate deliveries, which you always want to strive for when casting to wary bonefish.

In addition to a longer front taper on the fly line, you will also want relatively long leaders for bonefish. For most conditions, the minimum length is the same as the length of most rods, about nine feet. If it gets very windy you may have to shorten your leader to something like six feet. But if it's a dead-calm day and the fish are tailing in water as shallow as a sidewalk puddle, you may have to use a leader twelve to fourteen feet long. Because you have to adjust to conditions that can change by the hour, you want a leader that can be quickly and easily modified. Following the advice of Lefty Kreh, who originated the system, I recommend the loop-to-loop method. Regardless of length, a leader has to be tapered correctly to turn over properly, and to keep its construction uncomplicated I use Lefty's simple 4-3-2-1 formula. Longer or shorter leaders can be made by simply changing the length of the different sections, but as a general guideline your leader can consist of a four-foot section of 25-pound-test mono, followed by three feet of 20-pound, two feet of 15-pound, and one foot of 12- to 6-pound-test mono. As wary as bonefish may be, tippet size doesn't seem to be all that critical and for most situations 12- to 8-pound-test for the terminal section works just fine. But if it's extremely calm and clear you may have to drop down to something like 6-pound-test.

Bonefish feed on a wide variety of bottom-dwelling organisms such as shrimp and crabs, and it's no wonder that a great many fly patterns have been developed to imitate these food sources. But despite this diversity, there are two features that most bonefish flies have in common. One is size. Bonefish have comparatively small mouths and most flies are tied accordingly. However, there is a relationship between fly size and the size of the fish you find in different areas. With the exception of the large bonefish that move onto the flats on the east side of Bimini in January, South Florida gives up some of the world's biggest bones. Shell Key, on the Florida-Bay side of Islamorada, the Arsnicker Keys, and Biscayne Bay are prime areas for trophy fish, and the most commonly used bonefish flies in the Florida Keys tend to be somewhat larger than those used in the Bahamas, the Caribbean, or at Christmas Island. Keys patterns are generally tied on size 2 or 4 hooks and aren't more than 2 1/4 inches long. Outside the U.S., smaller flies tied on size 6 or 8 hooks seem to work better. As a rule, it's easier to cast a smaller fly closer to the fish without alarming it.

Bonefish will take offerings suspended below the surface but they are primarily bottom-feeders, and that's where you want to get the fly. This relates to the second characteristic bonefish flies have in common. To eliminate fouling problems, many flies are tied inverted so their hook points ride up. This can be accomplished by tying the fly bend-back style or by securing bead-chain or lead eyes on the top of the hook shank. With weight on the top side, a fly will flip over and the hook point will face away from the bottom.

Chico Fernandez is not only an expert with the fly rod, he is also a master at the fly-tying vise and has originated a number of bonefish patterns that have become true classics. A principal dietary item of bonefish is the snapping shrimp, and Chico's appropriately named fly is a deadly imitation. His Bonefish Special is also a top producer. Bob Nauheim, a West Coast fly fisherman with vast international experience, developed the Crazy Charley. He originally tied this fly for the flats around Andros Island in the Bahamas, but it will take bones as far away as Christmas Is-

Varieties of the famous "Charlie" pattern that have proved successful for bonefish.

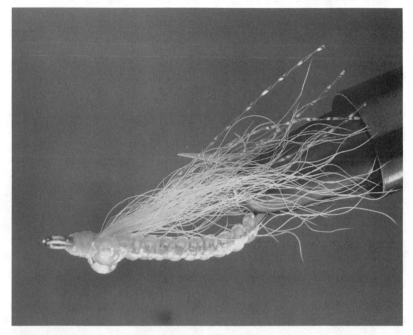

Pearl-Eye Charlie

Lead-Eye Charlie

Bead-Eye Charlie

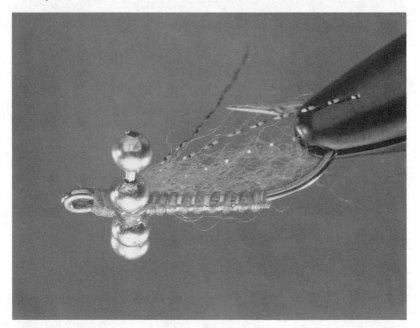

Four-Eyed Charlie

Bearded Charlie

land. And by all means, do not overlook Rick Ruoff's Backcountry Bonefish Fly; with its unique configuration of deer-hair and lead eyes, it has proved itself as one very potent offering for bonefish.

Of course, despite their proven ability to entice fish, these flies are only as good as the angler using them. For bonefish (and this applies to most fish on the flats), a deft touch is required when manipulating the fly. Even though they have come onto a flat to feed, these fish are wary. Shallow water offers little protection, and bonefish will flush at the slightest provocation. A fly that is retrieved too quickly can alarm a bonefish that might otherwise have been inclined to eat it. There is no one retrieve that works best under all circumstances, but as a general rule a fly that is manipulated slowly—only two or three inches at a time—will draw the most strikes. An erratic, stop-and-go retrieve can also trigger the bonefish's feeding instincts.

Presentation is also critical. Flies do not give off scents, at least not any that are natural to the fish's environment. Therefore, the fly must be presented in such a way that the fish can see it. Never cast a fly behind a fish. Obviously, it can't be seen, but worse yet, if the fly's landing is heard or its presence somewhat detected, the fish will bolt immediately. I've had this happen even when casting to fairly large sharks. Many predators take their prey unawares by coming up on it from the rear, and if you want to frighten a fish in shallow water, just make a little disturbance behind it.

One of the ideal situations with bonefish, or permit for that matter, is when the fish are actively feeding. A fish feeding in very shallow water is said to be "tailing"; with its head inclined toward the bottom a portion of its tail fin is exposed above the surface. When a fish is probing the bottom its field of vision is restricted and the fly must be cast close enough to be detected. Most experts would agree that the fly should land one to three feet ahead of the fish. When bones or permit are cruising a flat, however, the standard practice is to place the fly approximately eight to twelve feet in front of the fish.

Although it's not always possible, watching a bonefish go through the entire process of taking your fly is especially exciting. Just before nailing the fly, a bonefish's actions are remarkably similar to a cat about to pounce. A cat will flick its tail and sometimes wiggle its hindquarters, and the bonefish's tail will vibrate with excitement. However, there are times when factors such as cloud cover or a wave-rippled surface make it impossible to get a clear picture of exactly what is going on. In these situations you have to rely primarily on your sense of touch to detect the strike.

As you should always do, begin the retrieve with the rod pointed low to the water. In fact, if you're wading, it's not a bad idea to poke a few inches of the rod tip below the surface. The object is to maintain as tight a line as possible so that you'll be able to detect the slightest resistance to the fly's movement. If the fish swims toward the fly and then stops, it's a good bet that it's going to take it. But if you can't actually see this, one thing you can do is make a long strip. If the fish has taken the fly, the line will come tight and in most cases the hook will already be set. Some anglers raise the rod tip, but this creates slack that must be removed before setting the hook. Furthermore, if the fish hasn't taken the fly, you'll want to immediately impart action but you can't until all the slack is removed. The best way to proceed is to keep your rod tip low. The worst-case scenario is a refusal, but at least you can continue to manipulate the fly. When a bonefish does take your offering, your outfit seems to come alive as you feel the pressure of the arching rod and the speed of the line as it races through your hand. It's a sensation that will keep you coming back for more.

The proper rod and line weights for bonefish will vary according to location and conditions. In Florida, where bones can average six to eight pounds, 8- and 9-weight outfits are often the best choices. If the water is very shallow, requiring an extra-subtle presentation with a smaller fly, a 6- or even 5-weight rig would be a more appropriate choice. These lighter outfits are also more fun with the smaller two- to four-pound bones that predominate in some areas of the Bahamas and Caribbean. However, if the wind kicks up it may be necessary to step up to an 8- or 9-weight.

Tarpon

Many fish may shine and flash but only one has earned the designation "silver king." This, of course, is the tarpon. In the sense that they provide just about everything one could ask for in the name of sport, tarpon are truly horn-of-plenty gamefish.

In shallow water, tarpon can be very difficult to approach and just as wary as any bonefish. But unlike the lockjaw-prone permit, the silver king will usually take a well-presented fly. And when you have set the hook in one, a multitude of sensations combines to produce what many consider the ultimate experience in saltwater fly fishing. There is no in-shore gamefish that can match a tarpon's aerial displays. If you want to be humbled, just have 100 or so pounds of twisting, gyrating muscle explode from the surface, only to come crashing down again like a log being shot from a chute. Even the smaller specimens under fifty pounds are great fun on 8- and 9-weight outfits. You can even scale down to 5- or 6-weights for "babies"—10 pounds and under—but to handle big guys over 100 pounds you'll have to start with 11-weight gear.

With many gamefish, to stand a good chance of scoring with fly-fishing gear you often have to resign yourself to traveling outside the continental U.S. Not so with tarpon on the flats. Though they are found in many tropical regions, such as the Caribbean, Mexico's Gulf Coast, Central and South America, and even parts of Africa, some of the best tarpon fishing is in South Florida. The most consistently productive areas extend from lower Biscayne Bay in Miami through Key West and the Dry Tortugas, and along the Gulf Coast near Homasassa.

They say that springtime turns a young man's fancy to thoughts of love, but if it's flats tarpon you have your heart set on, spring is the time of year to go to Florida. When the water temperature on the flats reaches the mid 70s, the main migratory run up through the Keys starts—usually in late March, and the season lasts through August. The prime month for the big boys over 100 pounds (and guide bookings bear this out) is May. Both May and June are excellent times to catch big tarpon around Islamorada and Marathon.

The demarcation weight for small tarpon is generally about fifty pounds, and while larger specimens are available almost everywhere the species is found, the junior-class fish seem to favor certain areas over others. Small and medium-size tarpon are uncommon on Florida's west coast north of Tampa Bay. Your best bet is Florida Bay and the brackish areas in the Everglades. Some of the mosquito drainage ditches and canals in the Everglades can be especially productive.

They may be smaller, but on scaled-down outfits juvenile tarpon can be every bit as challenging as their big brothers. Consider, for example, their penchant for hanging around the mangrove shorelines of Florida Bay near Flamingo. During high spring tides from late spring to early fall, smaller tarpon will lie in wait among the mangrove branches, ready to ambush prey unfortunate enough to pass their way. When you make a good presentation the strike is often instantaneous, but your casting skills will have to be well honed. Just like snook in similar circumstances, these tarpon are not going to come out very far to chase prey. They don't have to, so you're going to have to put the fly within easy reach, often not more than a foot or so in front of them.

This might require a horizontal or sidearm cast to get the fly under low-lying branches. This type of cast is useful for two other reasons. It can minimize the glint of sunlight reflecting on the line, which can easily spook fish. And, because the fly is delivered only a foot or two above the surface, you get a more delicate presentation compared to a standard overhead cast, in which the fly drops from a height of ten feet or more. To make a sidearm cast, begin the back cast in the normal manner, but when almost all the line is lifted off the water, tilt the rod to the right and keep it nearly parallel to the water. The power stroke on the forward cast is made in the same parallel plane, with the tip of the rod remaining below your head.

Assuming that you have done all this correctly and have succeeded in getting one of these tenacious slabs of silver to nail your fly, you are still confronted with the formidable task of getting it out of its snag-infested lair. Expect to lose some flies in the process.

Generally speaking, the most productive flies for tarpon on the flats are relatively small, sleek patterns from 1 3/4 to about 4 inches in length. Along Florida's west coast and for those times when tarpon appear to be resting, lying motionless just below the surface, larger streamers from 5 1/2 to 7 inches long can be more to their liking.

From the standpoint of bodily proportions, the tarpon's mouth is large; a big fish looks as if it could easily engulf a volleyball. For larger tarpon, flies are tied on hooks that range in size from 3/0 to 5/0. There are some expert anglers, however, such as Rick Ruoff, who don't use hooks larger than size 2/0 because they feel that it's too difficult to effectively penetrate a tarpon's hard mouth with a larger hook. When you're after smaller tarpon, scale down the hook sizes accordingly. For example, size 1/0 and 2/0 work well for fish in the twenty- to fifty-pound class. Size 1 and 2 hooks are good for juvenile fish around 10 pounds, and for the small fry under five pounds you can drop down to a size 4 hook.

In terms of fly patterns, there seem to be as many variations as there are anglers tying them. But you have to start somewhere, and for most clear-water flats you can't go wrong with Steve Huff's or Rick Ruoff's tarpon flies. These two gentlemen are acknowledged to be among the finest guides in the Keys and their tarpon flies are always in great demand. The Stu Apte Tarpon Fly and the Cockroach are also excellent patterns. These are sparsely tied flies, generally about 2 1/4 to 4 inches in length, with six to eight saddle or neck hackles tied at the rear of the hook shank. Many expert tarpon fishermen prefer neck hackles because they flare better and are less prone to fouling around the hook as sometimes happens with softer saddle hackles. The collars—palmered hackle on the Stu Apte Fly and squirrel tail on the Cockroach—are tied immediately in front of the tails and are slanted rearward so they lay back toward the tails. The remainder of the hook shanks can be left bare or built up with fly-tying thread. The important point is that these patterns don't foul when cast, something you want to avoid at all costs. You will seldom, if ever, find a gamefish that will hit a fouled fly that has its feathers wrapped around the bend of the hook.

Of course, even a well-constructed fly must be worked in such fashion as to draw the fish's interest, and for tarpon this generally involves a slow, tantalizing retrieve. Some have described it as a sort of pause-and-jerk method whereby the fly is moved in 6- to 12-inch spurts.

Because of where I live, I spend considerably more time throwing flies at members of the tuna family than I do at tarpon. Tuna food swims much faster than the bait that tarpon normally pursue on the flats. Therefore, I'm in the habit of stripping line at a fairly quick pace. But this isn't what you want to do when tarpon fishing, and I have to constantly remind myself to slow up the retrieve.

Many years ago, working a flat off Belize with Chico Fernandez, I received a bit of advice that has served me well whenever I'm after tarpon. We came upon a pair of eighty-pound tarpon lazily cruising the edge of a narrow channel that divided the flat. It was my turn to cast and I got off a good presentation, about seven feet in front of the lead fish. It turned toward the fly, followed it for three or four seconds, and then veered off. Chico read my puzzled expression and simply said, "Too fast, man." When he saw me looking for another fly he told me there was nothing wrong with the one I had on. In essence, he advised me to let the fly do the work: "Those are fine, premium-grade hackles—let them breathe in the water. Work it nice and slow." Since then, whenever I manipulate a fly for tarpon, I think about trying to make the wing undulate in an easy up-and-down motion, and this has helped slow down the pace of my retrieve.

Whenever possible, you should watch both the fish and the fly and be prepared to make adjustments as necessary. As a rule, when a tarpon starts tracking your fly you shouldn't stop or slow down the retrieve. In fact, sometimes suddenly speeding up the fly's movement will induce a strike. It's as if the fly is trying to escape, and just like a cat pouncing on an object you're trying to pull away from it, the tarpon isn't about to let it get away.

Like baseball pitchers, tarpon fishermen have to be concerned with the "strike zone." Only in this case it's not established by a set of man-made rules. It refers instead to the area where the fish can easily en-

The author displays a Yucatan tarpon he took while fishing at Paradise Lodge in Mexico. *Photo by Lou Tabory.*

gulf the fly. And even more so than in baseball, this zone is quite restricted; it's only about a foot on either side of the tarpon's head.

When casting, you want to present the fly so it can be worked into this zone without alarming the tarpon. As is true with bonefish, the surest way to spook a tarpon, especially in shallow water, is to cast behind it. The effect is like someone coming up behind you unawares and suddenly shouting in your ear. In the predator-prey relationship, it's always the former trying to sneak up behind the latter. Even if you were behind the fish and managed to make a cast well in front of it without frightening it, it would be totally unnatural to strip the fly and have it come toward the tarpon. Nature doesn't work that way. Prey doesn't charge headlong into a predator that's going to devour it. If a tarpon encounters such a freaky scene it will more than likely quickly vacate the area.

In a similar vein, if you happen upon that peculiar ritual known as

Tarpon rolling on the surface are a magnificent sight. *Photo by Lefty Kreh.*

"daisy chaining," in which the fish swim directly behind one another in a circular pattern, avoid casting the fly in the center because it will frighten the school. Make the cast so the fly lands outside the circle alongside one of the fish. In this position the tarpon can approach the fly from the side.

They may not have teeth as we think of them, but the inside of a tarpon's mouth has been likened to a cinder block, making them one of the most difficult fish to sink a hook into. This is one species to which I wouldn't even bother casting a fly unless the hook was properly sharpened. If you want to get more than just a few jumps out of the fish, the fly's hook is going to have to penetrate, and that means it must be razor sharp. (Refer back to the end of Chapter 1 for the hook-sharpening process.)

Even with a sharp hook, effectively sticking a tarpon is not an easy task, and opinions are divided as to how one should go about it. Because situations vary, it's safe to say that there is no single best strategy. However, there are some guidelines that should be noted.

The strike zone is designated as the area lying to the side of a tarpon's head rather than directly in front of it because one of the best opportunities for an effective, positive hook-set is when the fish takes the fly from the side. As it closes down on the fly and begins to move off with it, the fly will drag against the tarpon's mouth, with a good chance that it will lodge in the soft tissue at the corner of the mouth.

Part of what makes tarpon fishing so exciting is that most of the time you can actually see the fish eat the fly. But if you're not accustomed to this type of visual drama, your first course of action may not be the best one. The almost instinctive response is to strike immediately, but most experienced guides recommend that you pause momentarily and not strike until you feel the line come really tight. On the other hand, you don't want to wait too long, or the tarpon will eject the fly by blowing it out of its mouth. If the fish is tracking the fly and coming straight at you, maintain your stripping rhythm because the tarpon has determined the fly's swim rate and has timed its attack accordingly. As mentioned previously, if a change is made it should be to increase the fly's speed, making it look like it's making a frantic effort to escape. Sometimes this is sort of a last-ditch effort when a tarpon has followed the fly quite a distance but seems reluctant to take. In most cases, it's a better move than having the tarpon keep coming closer and closer until it sees the boat and spooks. In any case, when the tarpon opens its mouth and swallows the fly, stop stripping for a second or two to give the fly time to travel farther back in the tarpon's mouth. This also makes for a good hook-set.

Keep your rod tip low as you retrieve the fly. Striking strategies vary, but as a general rule it is good practice to strike by pulling back hard with your line hand while simultaneously sweeping the rod sideways. Rotating the rod sideways makes it easier to recover line if the fish misses the fly, because the fly hasn't been pulled very far from the strike zone. Repeatedly snapping the rod straight up is not the way to proceed. Think about it for a second. That's usually how anglers try to free their flies from snags. But in this instance the object is to make the fly stick, not work loose. Furthermore, if you snap the rod up and back, you may very well jerk the fly from the water. By sweeping the rod sideways, your offering is not so far out of position that the tarpon can't get a second shot if it misses the fly the first time.

Once you have hooked the fish, hold the line tight and maintain as much pressure as you feel the class tippet can withstand. At this point you have to be ready to react quickly to the tarpon's next move. Most of the time the fish will start to swim off, and that means that you'll have to ease up on the pressure. You will also have to clear any loose line lying on

Lefty Kreh fights a tarpon on Rio Colorada in Costa Rica. *Photo courtesy of Lefty Kreh.*

deck. There are times, however, when a tarpon doesn't move off right away. If this happens, do not try to fight the fish by hand-stripping line. What you should do instead is wind any loose line back onto the reel. Be prepared for sudden movements, because they are sure to come in one form or another.

Naturally, the more you try your hand at this, the more adept you become. And I can't think of any practice sessions that are more fun.

Permit

Before I ever had a chance to fish for permit, Mark Sosin told me to think of all the challenges involved in bonefishing and then to double them; only then would I begin to understand permit. When I think about my experiences with this deep-bodied trophy of the flats, I would have to say that, if anything, Mark's assessment may have been an understatement.

Permit are so wary that sometimes they seem the angling equivalent of chasing rainbows. Even when you manage to get a clear view of a permit, it's difficult to establish actual contact. Although you can encounter them on many of the same flats frequented by bonefish, permit are not nearly as abundant. Even in regions where there are fairly good populations, such as on the flats in Mexico's Ascension Bay, the fish spook so easily that many of the native guides refer to them as "espantos," which translates as "spirits." If you have ever tried to put a fly in front of one of these paranoid, erratic, sickle-finned phantoms of the shallows, you'll agree with that description. Comparing permit to bonefish will give you some idea of what you are up against. Permit are almost as fast, they grow considerably larger, are much more powerful, far more elusive, and much less inclined to take a fly than are bonefish.

It is this last characteristic that has caused fly fishermen the most frustration. Since the end of World War II, when saltwater fly fishing began to come of age in south Florida, there have been countless instances of expert anglers making flawless presentations only to come up empty-handed because the permit refused their offerings. There were times when a permit would rush a fly like a kid going for candy, but they were so rare as to be considered once-in-a-lifetime events.

The situation started to change, however, as innovative fly tyers developed patterns designed to "match the hatch." The "hatch" in this case consists of crabs, one of the permit's favorite foods. Bonefish, tarpon, and redfish also love crabs, but, unlike permit, they're also very willing to strike flies that simulate other food sources. Maybe that's why no one ever felt a strong urge to devise a special crab pattern for these fish. But it's a different story with permit; time and again they have shown a definite reluctance to strike patterns that typically produce well on other species.

Because permit are such a prized species, however, it was inevitable that fly fishermen would start tying patterns aimed specifically at them. Two of the earliest pioneers were Keys guides, Nat Ragland and Harry Spear. Their Puff Fly and Mother of Epoxy were among the first patterns that took permit with any degree of consistency. Instead of precisely imitating crabs, these flies were designed to simulate the movement of a crab trying to elude a predator. Crabs can't out-swim the fish that pursue them; their only alternative is to dive for the bottom and that's exactly what they do.

The credit for the first realistic crab imitation properly belongs to John Barr, Jim Brumgault, and George Anderson, who developed the highly successful McCrab. But this wasn't the end of it. With most fly patterns, refinement is a never-ending process, and tyers are continually trying to make improvements. In the case of the original McCrab, a major drawback was the deer-hair body. For many tyers, spinning deer hair around a hook shank isn't particularly easy. More important, deer hair is naturally buoyant, a quality totally out of character for a fly that you want to sink quickly. It was only fitting that Del Brown, one of the world's most successful permit anglers (he has the numbers and the records to justify this accolade), developed what has so far proved to be one of the best permit flies ever, a pattern he calls the Merkin. It has everything you could ask for in a permit fly. Unlike some other patterns, it is easy to tie (the body consists of rug yarn, which is much less trouble to work with than deer hair), easy to cast, and, most importantly, sinks quickly and at the same angle as a crab diving for the bottom.

Permit are often larger than bonefish, and flies for permit should be tied on size 1 or 1/0 hooks. Nine- and ten-weight rods matched to weight-forward floating lines are preferred for most conditions. Leaders can be the same length as for bonefish and reds (about ten feet) but you'll probably want to go a heavier class tippet, such as 12-pound-test. To increase the odds of hanging onto your prize, experts like Del Brown and Steve Huff recommend tying the fly to the tippet with a strong loop connection such as a five-turn Surgeon's Knot.

Perhaps more than with any other species, presentation and retrieve have to be just right to fool a permit. The ideal situation is to find feeding fish; they'll be probing the bottom with their heads down and are not as likely to see you and take off. But to catch a permit you have to make it see your fly, so you'll have to put it right on the fish—about one to three feet in front of its nose. This might spook the fish, of course, but it's a chance you have to take; if the fly doesn't land nearby, the permit probably won't see it, and it can't eat what it doesn't see. When a permit is cruising on a flat, you have to lead it by casting approximately ten to fifteen feet in front of it.

The next step probably violates all your instincts, but the best retrieve is often no retrieve at all. Remember, you want to simulate the action of a crab when it realizes a permit is trying to eat it. It doesn't try to bolt away because that's futile. Instead, it dives to the bottom and if it gets there it remains practically motionless. This is what you want to do with a crab pattern. Strip until the fish sees the fly and then let it drop straight to the bottom. Unless the permit begins to move off in another direction without the fly, don't move the fly until you feel the fish pick it up. When you think it has, slowly pull on the line. If you feel any resistance, strike sharply with your line hand and sweep the rod sideways. A permit's mouth has a texture something like soft leather. It's fairly easy to penetrate with a hook and, once in, the hook tends to stay put.

The prime time for permit in the Keys ranges from late February to May. Spring tides are best. Because of their much larger girth, permit are normally found in deeper water than bonefish. They frequently cruise the outside edges of a flat where the water depth may be three to five feet or more. Since crabs are their favorite food, they seem to prefer rocky or coral bottoms where these crustaceans are more abundant. Clear days and cloudless skies make it easier to see fish.

Fly fishermen normally abhor the wind, but a stiff breeze in the range of ten to twenty knots is often helpful when pursuing permit, because this creates surface chop that makes the boat less visible. However, it's another reason why you want to have your casting skills down pat. Unless you can afford to spend considerable time on the flats, you can't expect to get shot after shot at permit, and when the precious opportunity presents itself you'll have to be ready to meet what many consider to be the supreme challenge of the flats. Instead of "here today, gone tomorrow," a better characterization of permit is "here this instant, gone the next." You usually have one cast to a permit, so you'd better make it count.

OTHER GAMEFISH FOUND ON AND AROUND THE FLATS

Redfish

For years, the red drum, or redfish, was overlooked by many fly fishermen. Bonefish, tarpon, and permit grabbed the limelight and visiting anglers seldom gave reds much attention. It was different with the locals, however. From Texas to Florida, anglers who fished over shallow grassy bottoms, oyster bars, and mud flats knew the redfish as a bulldog-tough fighter considerably more approachable than most other skinny-water species.

Unlike most flats fish, redfish are highly prized as table fare and their stocks were nearly wiped out by commercial netters. But in the last few years the situation has improved enormously, thanks to conservation laws, and reds are abundant as ever. In a two-pronged effort to manage this fishery, both Texas and Florida have banned commercial fishing for reds and have tightened up sportfishing regulations. In addition to licensing and stamp requirements, Texas has a daily bag limit of three fish between twenty and twenty-eight inches. In Florida, it's one red a day between eighteen and twenty-seven inches and there is a closed season from March through April.

As might be expected, the rejuvenation of redfish stocks has rekindled interest in them, particularly among fly fishermen looking for a quality flats fishery. In Texas, redfish in the shallows have been likened to the Lone Star State's version of bonefish. But redfish are much more accessible than bonefish. Reds are plentiful along the Florida panhandle and on both the Atlantic and Gulf coasts. Moving west to Texas, reds can be found in shallow water along most of the state's coastline from the Louisiana border to the tip of the Rio Grande. The most consistent fishing in Texas is in the spring and fall, but, barring unstable weather fronts, redfish can be caught year-round. One of the best areas is the Laguna Madre region in south Texas between Corpus Christi and Port Isabel.

The redfish's diet is similar to that of bonefish—shrimp, crabs, and small baitfish—but because redfish frequent more turbid water, fly patterns for them are larger and bulkier than those normally used for bones. Standard saltwater patterns such as the Lefty's Deceiver, Clouser Minnow, and Seaducer in bright color combinations like red-and-orange and red-and-white in lengths from three to five inches have proved effective on redfish. Because these flies are often worked over grassy bottoms, snags can be a problem. To minimize this, keel-hook patterns and flies tied bend-back style should always be in your redfish assortment.

Like snook, redfish are one of the few flats fish that will regularly strike popping bugs on the surface and a great choice for this type of fishing is Ruoff's Backcountry Popper. But you have to be careful when you use a popper in very shallow water. A popper's primary appeal is based on the noise and surface disturbance it creates, two factors you normally try to avoid in skinny water. Therefore, a popper shouldn't be used indiscriminately on flats. At times, though, it can be very effective over grassy bottoms and in murky water. With a cruising red (in off-color water the only sign might be a wake) the popper should be cast about six to ten feet ahead of the fish so that it has at least a few seconds to settle before you begin working it. When you do pop it, work it gently so it will make soft popping sounds. Redfish will respond to such tactics, but you have to consider that, with their underslung mouths, nature designed them for bottom feeding. They frequently have difficulty engulfing a popper, and despite all the surface commotion you should hesitate a second or two before striking with your line hand.

Redfish are reputed to have poor eyesight that makes them easier to approach than bonefish, but you still have to execute a good presentation. On a gin-clear flat a bonefish with its keen eyesight can easily spot an offering ten to fifteen feet away. But that's not likely with a nearsighted redfish trying to pick out a meal in turbid, grass-strewn water. The trick here, as in other flats situations, is to cast the fly as close as you can to the fish without spooking it. With cruising reds, try to judge the required lead distance and the fly's sink rate so the offering will intercept the fish right in front of its nose.

A redfish's window of visibility is even more restricted when it's rooting headfirst along the bottom. Mud and silt often cloud the water around a feeding red. When the water isn't shallow enough to expose their bronze tails, keep an eye out for these telltale off-color areas because that's where fish are stirring up the bottom. Like a sow with its head in the feeding trough, a feeding redfish is pretty well occupied and you can approach to within a comfortable casting distance that will let you present the fly within a few inches of the fish. Allow the fly to settle and then retrieve with short jerk-and-pause strips.

Although redfish are willing feeders, you don't want to strike too soon. With a slack-free line in your hand, wait until you feel resistance and then strike with your stripping hand. Redfish aren't spectacular fighters; they don't make sustained, line-blistering runs and they never go airborne. But a red will put a good bend in the rod and stubbornly resist you when you try to pressure it your way. You seldom have to worry about the hook pulling out of a redfish's rubbery mouth.

Since most shallow-water redfish range from about two to ten pounds, an 8-weight outfit is ideal under most conditions. If it's exceptionally calm, a 7-weight could easily come into play. Break out a 9-weight if the wind picks up. Weight-forward floating lines are used most often, but when you're drifting over deeper flats or blind-casting to deep cuts a sinking-tip will put the fly into the strike zone. If you are using a relatively buoyant fly—a heavily palmered Seaducer, for example—an Orvis Hy-Flote Sink Tip with its fifteen-foot high-density taper will take the fly down without undue delay. If your fly is weighted it may be better to use an Orvis ten-foot sinking-tip that has a slower sink rate ($1^{1}/_{2}$ to $2^{1}/_{2}$ inches per second). A nine-foot tapered leader, basically the same as used for bonefish, is standard for redfish. As usual, you will have to adjust for wind, and if it starts blowing, shorten the leader to about seven feet.

Casting flies to red drum may lack the glamour associated with the Big Three, but for the growing ranks of anglers who have tried it, it's one of the few times they're happy to "see red."

The Great Barracuda

As the heading suggests, this fish is different from the California or Pacific barracuda, which we'll cover shortly. Both are in the Sphyraenidae family (barracudas) and their body shapes are nearly identical, but the similarities end there. The Great Barracuda grows considerably larger and is much more powerful than its slimmer California cousin. On tropical flats this saber-toothed predator is a superb gamefish that is often overlooked by fly fishermen, who encounter barracuda accidently or as an afterthought when other species aren't cooperating. I have a special affection for them, partly because a barracuda was the first gamefish I ever connected with on the flats and it initiated a love affair that continues to grow year after year.

It was a little more than twenty years ago that Lefty Kreh invited Lou Tabory, Pete Kriewald (Pete wasn't a captain back then) and me to come down to Miami and borrow his Hewes Bonefisher for a week of flats fishing at Key West and the Marquesas. Lefty couldn't join us, but the half-day he spent describing particular areas and giving us pointers was like a crash-course in flats fishing. One bit of advice was his insistence that we be on the alert for barracuda. It was January, and Lefty knew that this is prime time for 'cuda on the flats when cold fronts send water temperatures plummeting. Cool weather also drives off the bonefish and tarpon, two of the "glory" species we had hoped for, so initially there was a tinge of disappointment. But our first bouts with barracuda changed our minds, and from that time on I've never made the mistake of relegating them to the status of a second-rate gamefish. I've experienced many instances when they were tougher to fool than bonefish. And when you manage to stick a fly in one, you'll find that its fighting prowess can leave you breathless. A 'cuda will rocket into the air like a Polaris missile and I don't think there is a fish that can make faster tracks across a flat.

Appropriately enough, it was a seven-inch-long white Lefty's Deceiver that brought me my first barracuda. I spotted the fish lying over a white sand-pocket adjacent to a small channel where we were looking for tarpon. Back then I wasn't aware of the practicality afforded by the loop-to-loop leader system, so I had to go through the time-consuming task of tying on a leader with a short wire shock tippet. I was very lucky that day; the 'cuda not only remained stationary while I went through the re-rigging process, but to everyone's surprise it took the fly almost immediately after it landed about ten feet in front of it. Ten or twelve minutes later, after a few spectacular leaps and sizzling runs that created silt tracks resembling the exhaust trails from a jet, Lou managed to carefully grab the leader and release the nearly four-foot barracuda. Between the three of us, we caught eight more on that trip, but none were as easy as the first.

The biggest problem that fly fisherman have in presenting their offerings to barracuda has to do with speed. These toothy predators have a decided preference for artificials that hightail it through the water. A fast retrieve isn't too difficult to execute for spin fishermen, but when you're hand stripping line there's a limit to how fast you can make a fly go. To better the odds, Ray Donnersberger and George Cornish developed a long, slender FisHair fly patterned after the successful surgical-tube lure commonly used by spin fishermen. The fly simply consists of a sleek section of FisHair eight to ten inches long tied just in front of the bend in the hook. A small amount of rubber cement on the tail holds the strands together, makes it easier to cast into the wind, and adds to its snake-like motion as it's retrieved just below the surface. Fluorescent green, fluorescent red, orange, and white in combination with any of these colors all work well. Ruoff's Barracuda Fly is also deadly. It's designed to ride near the surface like a needlefish, one of the barracuda's favorite foods. Regardless of size (these fish can vary from "pencils" of just a few pounds to torpedo-class specimens), barracuda have large mouths and fly hooks can range from size 1 to 3/0. The smaller fish can easily be handled on 7- and 8-weight outfits, but for the "logs" 9- and 10-weights are more appropriate.

If you're serious about having it out with a 'cuda, a four-inch wire leader is a must. Heavy wire is not only hard to cast, it can also cause the fly to sink faster and deeper that you want it to in shallow water. I got carried away once, however, and used some ultra-fine wire. The barracuda didn't shy away from it, but I lost two good fish because they were able to bite through it. Since then I've become more realistic and secure my barracuda flies with wire testing at least 32 pounds.

Barracuda have great eyesight and they don't lack for anything in the hearing department, either. When one sees or hears you, the game is usually over right then and there. They can be unpredictable and you can get lucky, but to improve your chances you want to make careful presentations. And with barracuda, given their ultra-keen senses, this involves being able to execute fairly long casts—often seventy feet or more. 'Cuda don't tail like bonefish, permit, and reds. Like tarpon and snook, they often lie motionless, waiting to nail whatever prey comes their way. It isn't necessary to try to draw their attention because they are very well attuned to their surroundings. Instead, it's better to lead a barracuda by casting well beyond and in front of it. And, rather than trying to zip the fly through the water right from the start, it's often better to begin stripping fairly slowly. Then, when you think you have the fish's attention, you can speed up the retrieve. It's the familiar ploy of simulating the movement of a baitfish trying to flee, something that most predators simply can't resist.

On the flats, weight-forward floaters are the lines to go with, but blind-casting in deeper channels with sinking lines can get you hooked up with barracuda you never knew were there. I connected with one of my biggest 'cuda ever using this method in a deep cut between the flats on Ascension Bay. The fish was in the four-foot range, but I'll never know for sure. I had planned to release it anyway, but the inexperienced guide hastened the process when the fish was brought to the boat. Like sharks, barracuda have wicked teeth that can do a great deal of harm if you're not careful. My guide was aware of this, but apparently didn't know how to immobilize the fish so we could measure it before releasing it.

The same method used to boat and release tarpon applies to 'cuda, but you want to be even more careful because of the barracuda's teeth. Gaff the fish in the lower jaw, and pin its head to the boat's gunwale. If they fly isn't too deep inside the fish's mouth (in which case you should cut the leader as close to the fly as possible), remove it with a pair of pliers. There's an additional step that too many anglers ignore. This involves making sure the fish has enough strength to swim away on its own. Instead of just plopping it back into the water, lower it gently. Hold it with one hand on the tail and the other under its belly. If it's in good shape, the fish will move off right away. If not, help aerate its gills by moving it back and forth in the water. When it's ready it will swim out of your hands.

Snook

With more than a dozen species and subspecies and a high tolerance for different salinity levels, snook are widespread both geographically and in their choices of habitat. They are found in both the Atlantic and Pacific oceans from about mid-Florida down through Central and South America. They are absolutely a warmwater species and are very sensitive to temperature fluctuations, preferring a range between 70 and 85 degrees Fahrenheit. When conditions are to their liking, they'll inhabit a wide variety of locales from ocean reefs to brackish canals. As far as fly fishermen are concerned, brackish water and mangrove-studded shorelines are where you're most likely to tie into snook.

Their diet in these areas consists mostly of small baitfish and shrimp, which may explain their readiness to take such a potpourri of fly-rod offerings. Streamers, popping bugs, hair bugs, muddlers, and divers will all entice snook. Your choice of fly should match the snook's feeding patterns and habitat. For example, when casting up against mangrove keys, popping bugs are practical because they don't snag easily on submerged branches. Of course, if the snook aren't receptive you may have to go to streamers. But since a streamer is fished below the surface there is a greater likelihood of snags, and for this reason many snook patterns are tied with either wire or mono-loop weedguards.

One characteristic of snook that fly fishermen should tune into is their habit of lying in wait for prey to be swept their way. Since tidal currents carry shrimp, crustaceans, and small baitfish that can't swim

Snook. *Photo by the author.*

against the flow, it follows that stronger currents generally result in better fishing, and this is certainly the case with snook. Locating the specific areas where snook set up feeding stations is the tricky part. On the flats you should look for white holes, cuts, and channels. Along mangrove shorelines, points and pockets are key holding spots for snook. Long, probing casts from a drifting boat is a productive tactic because it provides the opportunity to cover extensive stretches of water. Those who have experience fishing for largemouth bass will find that snook exhibit a similar pattern of congregating together; where there is one, there are usually more. So if you hit a fish in a certain spot, it pays to work that area thoroughly.

Streamers such as Steve Huff's Backcountry Fly are good choices when making extended drifts because they can be worked through the water over a far greater distance than poppers. Some veteran snook anglers prefer patterns that are about three inches long. Most snook flies are unweighted, but size 1/0 hooks are commonly used, partly to help the flies sink; even though the water up against the mangroves may be only a few feet deep, a fly has to get down rather quickly for the snook to see it. To help prevent fouling, many patterns are tied "Keys style," as described in the section on tarpon. In fact, scaled-down versions of classic tarpon patterns make good snook flies. Favorite colors are yellow, red and yellow, yellow and white, yellow and grizzly, and red and black. For night fishing, which can produce some of the best action with snook, black patterns are particularly effective. The pause-and-jerk style of retrieve that's so effective on tarpon can also be deadly on snook. Strip the line in foot-long pulls with brief pauses to allow the feathers to "breathe."

Unfortunately, the snook's superiority as table fare and years of unchecked habitat destruction have resulted in a significant decline in South Florida stocks. While the situation is beginning to improve, fly fishermen who want the best chance to catch big snook should consider a trip to Costa Rica. Unquestionably, the best fly fishing for snook I've experienced has been at Bill Barnes's Casa Mar Lodge. There are no flats at Casa Mar, but all the other types of snook habitat are plentiful: structure-laden shorelines, canals, and brackish backwater lagoons. The snook will occasionally take poppers, but the most consistent fishing in Costa Rica is with sinking lines and streamers; it's essentially a scaled-down version of the region's famous deep-water tarpon fishing. In many places the water is only six to ten feet deep, but the strong current in the river mandates sinking lines. Sinking-tip lines are appropriate in the calmer backwaters, and don't overlook floating lines because there is good shallow-water snook fishing in a number of the lagoons. For most conditions an 8- to 9-weight outfit will serve you well in both Florida and Costa Rica.

Regardless of where you tie into them, snook are worthy adversaries. As with most structure-oriented species, once you hook one you'll have your work cut out for you trying to pull it away from its snag-infested haunt. The best tactic is to pressure the fish from cover by hand-stripping line. If you take the time to reel loose line back onto the reel, the fish will probably break you off or have you so tangled that you'll have to break it off. It's a contest you can't always expect to win and lost flies and broken tippets are all part of the game. Snook do not come easy. Maybe that's why there's a cadre of dedicated anglers who keep coming back for them.

Sharks

Shark fishing on the flats is very different from fishing for them offshore. Except for large rays or a partner who falls overboard, sharks are the largest critters you'll encounter in skinny water. Merely watching them in the shallows is thrilling. It can also be a little scary if you're wading, despite what we all know about fish being easily frightened on the flats.

Blacktip, lemon, and bonnet sharks are the most common in the Keys and that's where I had my first encounter twenty years ago. I landed, that is to say I brought it alongside the boat, a blacktip about four feet long, and since then I never pass up the opportunity to fish for sharks on the flats. Truk Lagoon and Christmas Island, both in the Pacific, are great spots for blacktip fishing. My guide at Christmas Island laughed at me because practically every time I saw a blacktip, no matter how small, I had to make a cast to it. And they are so eager there that most of the time they'll even take small bonefish flies. Of course, if you do this without a wire leader, you have to be prepared to sacrifice a lot of flies.

One of my fellow guests on a trip a few years back asked me why I was so keen on tossing flies to sharks. When I convinced him to give it a try and he succeeded in hooking one, his next question was if I had any extra wire leaders. Sharks have a bad reputation, some of it deserved, but a great deal of it is the product of unfounded myth. They are terrific gamefish, especially in shallow water.

Contrary to what some think, sharks are not all that easy to take on the flats, although the specimens in the far Pacific seem much less wary than those in the Keys. Sharks rely primarily on their sense of smell to locate food, and to get their attention you have to put the fly fairly close. This may take a little practice; being larger than most fish in the shallows, a shark covers a lot more distance in a shorter period of time. If the fly or the line lands too close or makes too much noise, even a big shark will spook.

Sharks have large mouths, but in shallow water you don't want to use very large hooks because your flies will sink too quickly and might get snagged on the bottom. I've found that hook sizes 1/0 to 3/0 provide ample hooking effectiveness. Fancy patterns aren't necessary; brightly colored flies that contain Flashabou or Crystal Flash will do the trick. A bright fly is also easy to see as it's being worked below the surface. Cast the fly alongside the eye of the shark so it catches the shark's peripheral vision and then retrieve it slowly. The take is often a blend of gluttony and fury.

Getting a shark to take your fly is only a small part of the challenge. Once a shark has your fly, you and your tackle will be subjected to long, powerful runs that few species can match. For smaller specimens, such as the baby blacktips at Christmas Island, bonefish tackle is adequate and a lot of fun. But for larger sharks—those that reach or exceed the five-foot mark—your outfit needs to be stout. A 12-weight isn't too heavy.

You can use pliers to remove a fly from a barracuda, but with a shark it's best not even to bother. A shark is likely to take the fly deep, and attempting to retrieve it is like trying to extricate a fork from a running garbage disposal. The safest course of action is to simply cut the leader.

WEST COAST INSHORE GAMEFISH

Calico Bass

Long popular with conventional and spin fisherman, calico bass are just beginning to draw the attention of West Coast fly rodders. They can be taken from the surf and in bays, but your best bet is to fish close to breakwaters, jetties, inshore reefs, rock outcroppings, and kelp beds. In addition to their vast geographical distribution (from the Channel Islands in the north to as far south as Magdelena Bay in Mexico), calicos also inhabit a greater variety of inshore habitats than just about any other species on the southern California coast. They can be caught year-round, but the months that fly fishermen want to pay close attention to are June and July. This is the calico's spawning period, which signals not only greater abundance but also bigger fish.

Calicos resemble freshwater bass and weigh, on the average, two to two and a half pounds. June and July are the best months to try for calicos over the four-pound mark, which Californians refer to as "bull bass." Unlike members of the tuna family, calicos (along with spotted bay and sand bass) are slow-growing fish. For this reason, the California Department of Fish and Game has instituted a twelve-inch minimum size limit for "keeper" bass. According to one of the department's bulletins on kelp bass, fishery biologists estimate that the average size of a year-old calico is only about four inches and that it takes between five and six years for it to reach the minimum legal size.

The best action with calicos seems to be during overcast conditions and at first light. If it's a bright, sunny day, the action can be over as early as eight in the morning. In dim light, I use dark flies with olive, black, or burgundy hackles. Calicos also show a preference for hot pink, so I always have a few flies tied in this color. Blanton's Whistler series, Lefty's Deceiver, and the Sardina are excellent patterns, and because calicos have big mouths your flies can be tied on size 3/0 to 5/0 hooks. Most of the action is subsurface, so sinking lines are what you'll need.

There are occasions, though, when calicos will feed on top, and when they do you can have a lot of fun with a floating line and a popper or slider. The surface action with calicos is generally during first light and normally doesn't last long, but you can prolong it if you have some chum in the form of live anchovies.

Some time ago, while fishing the jungle rivers of Costa Rica, I came up with a new twist for a slider-style popper, which I call the Jungle Jester. It combines a surface slider with a tube-fly configuration. The idea occurred to me while I was "bass bugging" for a tough, toothy, snag-loving river rogue called the machaca. Although its origin was far removed from California, the Jungle Jester is an excellent calico fly.

The cork head can slide up along the tippet away from the hook, making it nearly impervious to the ravages of toothy fish. The tube-fly design lets you change hooks while keeping the same body. This can be a very handy option when you want to adjust for different species or conditions, and if a hook is damaged it can be replaced without having to sacrifice the slider along with it.

Another convenient feature is that, since the materials are tied to a tube glued into the cork body, the fly can constructed in various lengths without having to increase or decrease the size of the cork. On conventional poppers the hair and feathers are bound to the hook shank, which means that the bug's length is in part a function of hook size. And since the hook is cemented into a conventional popper, changing the hook size usually means changing the size of the popper body. With a tube-fly configuration, however, it's possible to tie a relatively long fly without enlarging the size of the slider's head section. This keeps the fly's bulk to a minimum, which in turn makes it easier to cast.

Finally, the Jungle Jester's tapered head can draw strikes from fish that are normally not too interested in poppers. This has been the case with the popular "three Bs" of southern California coastal fishing: bass, barracuda, and bonito. With a standard popper, the variations in surface disturbances are somewhat limited. You can work it fast or slowly, create big pops or mild slurps. With the slider you can do all this and more. By snapping the line back sharply, you can make the blunt head push water and create a relatively loud and visible surface disturbance. But because it's streamlined, a slider can be worked considerably more quietly than a popper. And unlike a popper, it can be worked across the water with a zig-zagging motion that will draw strikes from fish that are not too keen on taking surface offerings.

With West Coast bonito, calico bass, and Pacific barracuda, I have found that the slider will induce more strikes than poppers by a two-to-one margin. The slow-to-moderate action of the slider as it meanders across the surface often proves irresistible to calicos and barracuda. Calicos will sometimes come up from the kelp stringers to strike it, while barracuda will track it for some distance on the surface and then suddenly explode on it. The bonito are the fastest of the three; they seem to come out of nowhere and all you generally see is a flash followed by a big boil on the surface. Friends who have used the Jungle Jester back East have reported good success with surface-feeding stripers and bluefish.

Bonito

The Atlantic bonito (*Sarda sarda*), Atlantic little tunny (*Euthynnus alletteratus*), also referred to as false albacore, and the Pacific bonito (*Sarda chiliensis*) are closely related. They are all members of a very distinguished family, the Scombridae, which includes the species commonly known as tuna. They are also much alike in terms of schooling, feeding, and fighting qualities. Like the species that scientists designate "true" tuna—albacore, yellowfin, and bigeye—bonito and little tunny are pelagic, migratory fish. Unlike their offshore cousins, however, they frequently pursue bait very near the coast, often within range of the shorebound angler. The nearly universal availability of bonito and little tunny is a significant factor in their growing popularity. In southern California, the bonito has introduced more people to saltwater fly rodding than any other fish. Unbelievable as it may seem in a region as densely populated as southern California, there is a relatively uncrowded world-class fishery right at the doorstep of Los Angeles in Redondo Beach's King Harbor.

Like other members of the tuna family, nature has brought bonito to an evolutionary stage of near-perfection. First of all, they rank among the fastest swimmers in the sea. In fact, because they are negatively buoyant, they never stop swimming. That's something to think about when you're gearing up for them: there is no such thing as a flabby bonito.

Second, because of this ceaseless movement, their energy requirements are very high. This doesn't mean that bonito will always eat anything that's thrown at them. Depending on conditions, they can get satiated and become downright selective. But when they do go on a feeding spree it's awesome to witness. In my home waters of King Harbor, which is one of the best bonito fisheries in the world, I've had the opportunity to observe these blue-and-green iridescent bullets for almost thirty-five years. When they find a tightly packed school of anchovies (referred to locally as a "meatball") the ensuing scenario is practically always the same. The terrified pod of baitfish is intercepted from practically every direction, and in a matter of only a few seconds everything is mopped up. During the early morning and late afternoon, when boat traffic is at a minimum, I have often seen bonito actually herd small packs of anchovies against the sea walls in the inner harbor and then methodically pick them off one by one. We have some tough neighborhoods on shore, but nothing like this.

Watching these metabolic dynamos feed has provided me with a number of clues as to how one should proceed with fly-fishing gear. The primary food source for bonito, both in the harbors and out in the open ocean, is anchovies. One of the factors that accounts for the great bonito fishing in King Harbor is the commercial bait receiver that stores huge quantities of anchovies in live-wells suspended in the water. A second important factor is that the water temperature in the harbor is considerably warmer than the outside ocean temperature. This is caused by the warm water discharged by the local Edison generating plant. Bonito are found in all southern California harbors where bait receivers are in operation, and the anchovies that are inevitably spilled, particularly when bait is transferred to fishing boats, often trigger wide-open feeding sprees.

At such times, when practically any reasonable offering will be immediately pounced on, you really do not get an accurate test of the effectiveness of any one pattern. Even when bonito are actively feeding,

Bonito. *Photo by the author.*

however, you will eventually find that some flies draw more strikes than others. The key factor is the size of a fly. The anchovies that are available to the sport-fishing fleet can vary in size from 2-inch-long "pinheads" to the larger "horse" specimens that may go 5 inches or more. To catch the most bonito, you should tie your flies on the small end of the scale, about 1¼ to 3 inches long. A common practice of novice saltwater fly rodders, particularly those who are making a transition from fresh water, is to tie flies that are heavily dressed and in lengths that resemble bottle washers. Don't do it.

A second relevant factor is that with smaller flies you can more effectively simulate the movements of injured and terrified baitfish. A relatively slow, jerk-and-pause stripping motion causes the fly to accelerate, dart, and then settle briefly in the water. This is typically the reaction of baitfish when bonito start smashing a school. Many are stunned or injured, and the predators will shoot by and pick off the wounded. Even the healthy bait make frantic, zig-zag movements in an effort to escape. Tying in bead-chain or lead eyes at the head of a fly will help give it the desired effect. This type of response would be difficult to simulate with long flies that tend to slide through the water in an eel-like fashion, and scaling down the size of your flies and using a slow to moderate retrieve with definite pauses between a series of strips is often the hot ticket with bonito. It is a common misconception that with bonito you always have to "burn" the fly through the water.

The largest hook size I generally use is 1/0. Most of my bonito flies are tied on sizes 1, 2, and 4 hooks. The flies themselves can be kept fairly simple. Lefty's Deceiver, small versions of Blanton's Whistler series, and the Tuna Tonic and Sardina patterns I developed several years ago are all very consistent producers.

Regardless of the pattern, it's important to tie the fly sparsely. Anchovies present a sleek silhouette in the water and the fly should do likewise. Many years ago, when I asked a commercial tuna fisherman what he thought the most productive color for a bonito lure was, without hesitation he answered blue and white. I have found that to be very good advice and I tie most of my patterns for bonito and other members of the tuna family with these two colors. Combinations such as white and yellow, green and white, and red and white are also very effective. With just the right angle of sunlight, you can sometimes see schools of baitfish flashing in the water, so adding a few strands of Mylar or Flashabou can enhance a fly's attractiveness.

Bonito have a full set of needle-like teeth, but you can still forego the use of a shock leader and tie the fly directly to the class tippet. The thin tippet will slide between the fish's teeth and cutoffs are rare. This doesn't mean that bonito aren't capable of inflicting damage on flies and fingers. It's good practice to carry along a pair of long-nose pliers; the "duck-bill" type with a slightly wider nose does a good job of extracting flies.

Years ago in King Harbor, many anglers used to land or boat their bonito by simply reaching down and grabbing the fish right in front of the tail. With the proliferation of seals in the harbor you must be careful. Seals are not intimidated by boats or humans and sometimes will grab fish right out of an angler's hand. If you are fishing from the rocks and can bring the bonito within reach, landing it by hand is generally safe. A landing net is much more prudent when you're fishing from a skiff. If they have a mind to, seals can also cause you a lot of trouble when you have a fish on. By themselves bonito are among the toughest fish you'll ever encounter. But when a seal the size of a baby whale decides it wants the bonito you've been battling, consider yourself lucky if you even get the fly line back intact.

When there is a great deal of chum present in the form of free-swimming anchovies, it's not uncommon to see ravenous packs of bonito boil the water as they tear into the baitfish, which may be suspended just below the surface. But you will still draw more strikes with sinking lines. Even whey they are busting bait on top, bonito seem to prefer a fly that is at least a few feet below the surface. If they change their minds and you happen to be using a fast-sinking line, it's still possible to keep the fly right near the surface by starting to strip as soon as it hits the water. More often than not, though, to draw strikes you will have to get the fly down.

For those who prefer floating lines and surface strikes, in addition to the Jungle Jester pattern there is a way to get top-water action by using a modification of the splasher rig used so effectively by spin fishermen. The standard splasher rig employs a floating chugger that may take the form of a wooden dowel, a water-filled plastic bubble, or even a sponge-rubber ball. This is followed by a four- to six-foot section of trailing leader with a fly tied on the end. The chugger is rhythmically pumped across the surface and the commotion draws the attention of the bonito, which strike the fly. With only a slight change in rigging, the system works equally well on fly gear.

Take a standard slant-faced cork popper approximately $1^1/4$ inches in length (these can be cut from $2^1/2$-inch tapered seine-net floats) and instead of a hook, glue a short piece of 30-pound mono with loops in both ends into the cork. The loops need only extend slightly beyond either end of the popper. The front loop is connected to the loop in the butt section (1 to $1^1/2$ feet in length) coming from the tag end of the fly line. The rear loop of the popper is connected to the loop in the class tippet with the fly tied at the tag end. The class tippet need only be about $2^1/2$ feet long. All you do is strip the cork body across the surface in a series of pops and get ready for some very exciting strikes at the trailing fly. If you are perched high atop the rocks, you get a good view of everything and it's often possible to see the bonito flash and boil on the surface just before

Bonito Splasher Rig

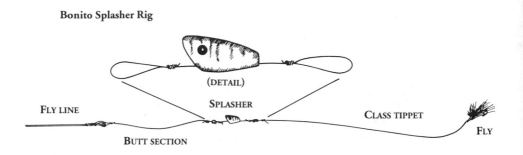

(DETAIL)

SPLASHER

FLY LINE

CLASS TIPPET

FLY

BUTT SECTION

they take the fly. The question inevitably arises concerning what happens in the event they hit the hookless popper. I have never had this happen. Worked by itself, the popper will occasionally draw strikes. But with a trailing fly, the cork is ignored by the bonito.

Since the popper body does present some bulk, I'd recommend a 9- or 10-weight rod. The Power Matrix-10 8-weight is great for casting streamers with shooting heads. But if the wind gets strong, you may want to step up to the Power Matrix-10 9-weight.

In southern California bonito are available on a year-round basis, but in the Northeast, the Atlantic bonito and false albacore are seasonal. The bonito generally make an appearance around mid-July, while the false albacore usually start to show in September. As the fall season progresses and water temperatures begin to plummet, this fishery draws to a close.

Just as with Pacific bonito, bait is the key factor in drawing these fish close to shore. Small offerings such as spearing and sand eels are prime targets for these eating machines, and when bait is carried along with incoming tides to locations like inlets and harbors, there is a good chance that bonito and little tunny will be in hot pursuit. Relatively sparse fly patterns such as Lefty Deceivers, Tabory's Snake Fly, and Glass Minnows are effective imitations of local baitfish. And, like their West Coast counterparts, most experienced bonito fishermen in the Northeast tie their flies on the small side, between 1¹/₂ and 4 inches long.

One difference between East and West Coast bonito is that the former tend to be leader shy. This is probably because Atlantic bonito often feed in clear, calm, shallow water. Under such conditions, an Orvis Clear-Tip line in conjunction with an eight- or nine-foot leader is an ideal setup. Eight- to twelve-pound-test class tippets are standard and these are tied directly to the flies with no shock leader. Bonito are real line burners, so whenever you fish for them you want a high-quality reel with a consistently smooth drag that can withstand long, scorching runs. The D-XRs or the new Odyssey series are the way to go for fish of this caliber. There are a few species anywhere that can test you and your tackle like bonito, and the beauty of it all is that they are so close to shore.

Pacific Barracuda

Pacific Barracuda are no different from other inshore species: they follow the baitfish. Depending on the availability of bait and the water temperature (they generally prefer a range from 62 to 70 degrees Fahrenheit), barracuda migrate to southern California waters from Mexico during the spring. Biologists say that the barracudas move offshore for their spawning activity during late spring and then begin moving shoreward again in late May and early June to feed on baitfish.

The barracuda is particularly suited to fly fishing. Unlike most gamefish on the West Coast, they do a great deal of their feeding on or near the surface. This is when you really want to be aware of surface disturbances or diving birds. You may even spot a few jumpers as they spring from the surface wahoo-style and pounce on bait. Sometimes you can actually hear them when they're chasing bait on the surface. In contrast to the loud, sharp crash characteristic of tuna, barracuda make a soft popping or slurping sound. Keep your ears open.

Early morning is the best time to hunt for barracuda around structure such as kelp beds and in the turbulent water near the points of breakwaters and jetties. Baitfish congregate in these areas and when barracuda are around they'll be in hot pursuit. Shallow zones adjacent to drop-offs can also hold good concentrations of barracuda. You can detect these areas by looking for abrupt color changes in the water. Where you see a change from a darker to a lighter hue, there's usually a break in the water temperature. This tends to attract forage fish such as anchovies and smelt. Later in the morning when the sun is brighter, the bait usually scatters and you have to begin hunting for barracuda again.

Since it generally isn't practical to do any fly fishing from a party boat, this type of inshore fly rodding requires a private boat or special charter. One familiar pattern that develops is for private boaters to congregate near the party boats. They do so for two reasons. First of all, they assume, and rightly so, that the party boat skipper knows where the fish are. Second, they want to take advantage of the party boat's chum line. This doesn't pose any problem as long as the private boats respect the party boat's position. As a rule of thumb, most of these professional skippers will consider any boat coming closer than 200 feet an encroachment. When you are in your own boat try to observe this courtesy and you will prevent a lot of hassles.

Most gamefish respond to chum, but none seem to do so quite as readily as barracuda. If you are serious about this fishing and have your own boat, by all means invest in a quality bait tank. Live anchovies are available for sale from a number of bait receivers located at major launching sites along the coast on a year-round basis.

As in any chumming situation, the key is consistency, not quantity. You are not trying to feed the fish. Instead, the object is to attract them and keep them milling around the boat. If you do it correctly, and another boat doesn't carelessly run across your chum line and put the fish down, you can keep barracuda and other gamefish in a striking mood for hours at a time. But the mistake that is so often made is failure to keep chumming once the action heats up. You will notice that on party boats there is always a deckhand positioned at the aft bait tank, methodically throwing live anchovies off the stern. As long as there is action this process continues uninterrupted.

A common practice for private boaters trying to take advantage of the party boat's chum is to anchor or drift down-current from the big boat. That way, the current will carry the bait toward them. This may work fine for other species, but barracuda tend to swim up-current, and so do anchovies. So unless there is a very strong current, it's best to position yourself off the party boat's bow.

Though nowhere near as formidable as the Great Barracuda of tropical waters, the Pacific species do have teeth that can easily sever your line. Years ago bait fishermen in southern California used single-strand wire, but today the fish seem more wary and most anglers tie their hooks directly to their monofilament lines and take their chances. Fly fishermen fare much better in this respect. You may lose a few fish, but in most instances the fish hasn't taken the fly so deep that it can bite you off. A short four-inch trace of light single-strand wire will prevent this and it doesn't seem to put the fish off. For added insurance I recommend using a hook with a fairly long shank. The Wright and McGill 66SS is a good choice. This is an offset hook but you can easily straighten it with a pair of pliers before tying on the material. For barracuda, sizes 1/0 and 2/0 work fine.

Back in the '40s and '50s, a feather jig was a very popular and effective lure for barracuda, and the hot colors were all-white, blue-and-white, and green-and-yellow. I use these same colors with a little Mylar tied in Deceiver-fashion and have had no difficulty drawing strikes from feeding barracuda. They like flash and you can add this by using silver Mylar piping as body material over the hook shank.

Although barracuda can be aggressive top-water feeders, the majority of the action is still sub-surface and sinking shooting heads are the primary lines. A moderate retrieve with intermittent stops and starts often produces the best results. Of course, when they are on top you want to go to a floating line and a slider pattern like the Jungle Jester. Snake this across the surface and be prepared for some explosive strikes.

Most of the local fish are somewhere between three and six pounds and in California there is a twenty-eight-inch minimum size limit. Smaller barracuda are referred to as "pencils," while the larger specimens are called "logs" or "snakes." They aren't long-distance runners like bonito but the larger ones will get into your backing and give a good account of themselves. Depending on the wind and whether or not you are casting sliders, an 8- to 10-weight outfit is all the tackle you need.

Yellowtail

With the possible exception of the increasingly rare bluefin tuna, yellowtail are without a doubt the strongest-fighting fish in southern California coastal waters. They are members of the hard-pulling jack family and close cousins to the amberjack. The yellowtail on the West Coast (*Seriola dorsalis*) range from Point Conception to Cabo San Lucas. In southern California most populations rarely range farther up the coast than Santa Barbara. In Mexican waters, the Coronado Islands just south of Point Loma, the Pacific side of Baja, and the Midriff Islands in the Sea of Cortez are all top producers.

Yellowtail

In addition to their fairly wide geographical distribution, an interesting characteristic of yellows is the different areas they will frequent. At times they may be found practically on the beach or far offshore under floating kelp patties. I've hooked them from shore in the Sea of Cortez. At the other end of the spectrum, I've found them milling around floating patches of kelp more than twenty miles offshore.

The really big yellowtail in the 100-pound-plus class are taken off Australia and New Zealand, but in local waters most fish generally range between eight and twenty pounds. Small fish in the 5- to 10-pound class are appropriately referred to as "firecrackers," and these small fry can quickly tear up inferior tackle. On a 9- or 10-weight outfit you will get quite a workout. Fish in the twenty-pound class on fly gear are simply awesome; break out the 12-weight tackle here. The late Harry Kime probably landed more of these brutes with a fly rod than anyone, and he rated them as one of the toughest adversaries in the sea. When you couple their tremendous fighting ability and staying power with the fact that they are a structure-oriented fish, it's easy to see why so few twenty-pound-plus yellows have been taken on fly gear.

Like calicos, yellowtails frequent what I like to refer to as "bad neighborhoods." Reefs, rock pinnacles, kelp beds, kelp patches, and oil rig platforms all attract yellows and there are few fish I know of that can put these obstacles to such good use when they are trying to free themselves. Once hooked, a yellowtail has an uncanny ability to go where it can cut you off or leave you hopelessly fouled. Amberjack also are great at this dirty trick but nowhere near as good at it as yellowtail. If there is only one lone obstacle in an area you can be sure that yellows will head for it.

A few years ago I signed on as a deckhand for a week-long whale-watching and ecology trip down along the Pacific side of Baja. Apart from being interested in the trip itself, I knew that there would be opportunities to fish from the skiffs that we used to transport naturalists and photographers to the various islands along the coast. I guess I'm probably the only person who has ever fly fished San Benitos Island, and what an experience that was! The yellows there attacked every fly I threw at them. But I didn't actually land many, because the island is choked with thick kelp and studded with rock pinnacles. The yellows knew every bit of structure and succeeded in getting to it better than seventy percent of the time. It even got to the point where I was losing entire fly lines that were dragged across the underwater ledges. This is one fish that can really humble me.

The yellow's favorite food is squid, but it also feasts on anchovies, mackerel, sardines, and even pelagic red crabs. Flies do not have to be exact imitations, but they should be tied to simulate the color and size of the bait in the area you are fishing. Although the warmer months can produce some of the best bites, if any of the aforementioned bait is available the yellows are not far behind and they can be caught year-round.

These fish can feed deep, sometimes too deep for fly fishing. On occasion I've resorted to 900-grain heads, but this is like casting telephone cable and I don't recommend it. Don't try to fish for them deeper than sixty feet. A moderately paced retrieve usually works well, but there are times when they want the fly to burn through the water. When a yellowtail hits, the fly just stops, period. Then be prepared for a line-blistering run and a slugfest that will soon have you drenched with sweat.

BAJA GAMEFISH

Roosterfish
One of the most exciting targets for the Baja-bound fly rodder is the roosterfish. The Latin name is *Nematistius pectoralis,* but its Spanish designations are *pez gallo, papagallo,* or simply *gallo* (rooster). The roosterfish is the turbocharged member of the jack family. Its high first dorsal fin sports seven elongated flexible spines that raise when the fish is aroused. The fin resembles a rooster's comb, hence the name. It also has a series of dark, bluish-black bands, two of which run diagonally across the fish's side all the way to the prominently forked tail.

The rooster inhabits tropical waters and is found only in the eastern Pacific and along the Baja coast down into Central America all the way to Peru. It has become a very popular sport fish in the Sea of Cortez and more recently in Costa Rica, where you can find roosters in even greater abundance. Relatively little is known about their breeding habits. The limited tagging studies conducted thus far indicate that they may spawn off Costa Rica along about mid-July.

Roosters can show a wide variation in size. You may find schools

A Baja roosterfish. *Photo by Chet Young.*

with junior-class fish going from two to twelve pounds, middleweights in the twenty- to forty-pound range and some real heavyweights that can hit the scales at over sixty pounds. In Baja, depending on the area, you can get into roosters from late February to September. At the Cape they may show as early as the latter part of February. Heading north up the East Cape and beyond, the peak months are April through July. Farther south in Central America and along the mainland coast of Mexico they are available all year long, but early spring sees some of the hottest action.

While it is possible to get roosters to take flies when they are actively feeding, more consistent results can be had by teasing the fish. There are two methods of doing this. Each has proved successful and both have their devotees. The more traditional method is to troll a hookless teaser plug on a flat line about fifty feet off the stern, working just outside the surf line; roosters often can be found feeding on schools of bait just a little beyond the surf. When a fish comes up to the teaser, the skipper or mate begins retrieving it and the angler casts a popping bug immediately behind the plug.

The popper can be made from cork or closed-cell foam. If you use the latter, a coating of five-minute epoxy enhances the finish and the hardened surface makes for better resistance when the popper is pulled through the water. An appropriate size is about the same as a Jungle Jester body, only in this case the front is slanted instead of bullet-shaped. The body can be about 1 3/4 inches long with a 3/4-inch diameter at the face. A size 3/0 or 4/0 hook is fine for roosters over the ten-pound mark. Some fly fishermen prefer yellow poppers, but I believe that the surface disturbance is more important than color. You may wish to experiment and draw your own conclusions.

The second teasing method is based on the premise that since roosters prefer live bait to anything else it makes sense to entice them with the real thing. Mackerel, mullet, goatfish, milkfish, and striped grunts will draw their attention, but a little teamwork is necessary to pull off the ruse successfully. The boat can be drifting or a very slow troll can be effected by taking the engine in and out of gear. The hookless live bait is tethered on a line and allowed to swim freely behind the boat at a distance that's within easy casting range of the angler. The person manning the teaser has to remain alert because a rooster can appear and strike the bait in a split second, and you don't want the fish to make off with the bait. In the event it does, even if you manage to get the bait it is usually pretty well mangled, and the rooster, having failed to secure a meal, loses interest.

The trick is to pull the bait away from the fish without allowing it to swallow it. Just as in sailfish-fishing, the moment the bait is jerked away the angler should cast the popper. Roosters don't tease as easily as sailfish and they may make only one or two passes at a bait and then turn off. But if you execute this maneuver properly, it may not even be necessary to pop the bug because the enraged *gallo* will often be on it the second it splashes down on the water. This is an exciting game and the person doing the teasing can have almost as much fun as the one doing the casting.

Cabrilla and Pargo

Even though these are distinct species, I put them together because they have a lot in common. In terms of basic body structure, feeding and fighting patterns, and habitat preference, they are quite similar. And the Mexicans use both terms to refer to a variety of fish that are closely related. Cabrilla, for example, is used to designate a number of bass-like fish that frequent rocky habitat along the middle to southern regions of the peninsula.

The most common member of this clan is the leopard grouper, sometimes called the *cabrillo pinto*. One of its main characteristics is the mottled pattern that runs along its sides. With some specimens hitting the scales at twenty-five pounds or more, it is also one of the largest members of the cabrilla family. Its close cousin, the spotted cabrilla, can grow even larger (to thirty pounds plus), and it will hold over sandy bottoms as well as rocks. The flag cabrilla is the tiny tot of the family, averaging only about a pound or two in weight. And the spotted sand bass is really the same fish that is found in southern California bays and harbors.

One of the areas where cabrilla proliferate is the Midriff Islands. These are located in the narrowest part of the Sea of Cortez, so the tidal action is very pronounced. These tidal surges create a mix of nutrient-rich water that predator fish find essential to their survival. When setting your sights on structure-oriented fish like cabrilla, it only makes sense to work the many tidal rips that prevail in these areas. These are not difficult to identify because the turbulence around rocky points and outcroppings is plainly visible when the tide is running. In this sense, it is very much like striper fishing along New England's rocky coastline.

Fishing for cabrilla is a casting game, and with proper boat handling the job is a whole lot easier. In many spots it may be possible to anchor, but the best results are when the skiff drifts slowly over a productive area. You cover more water that way and there can be advantages to returning to the same area; cabrilla sometimes respond better when they are subjected to intermittent presentations as opposed to anchoring the boat and hitting them with a barrage of casts. Besides, when the tide is running strong it isn't always possible to anchor. If one spot is producing very well, a better tactic is to leave the motor running and have the guide hold the skiff in the current so you can make repeated casts to the same area.

In many places along the rocky shore the depth will be between twenty-five and thirty feet. This, coupled with the strong tidal surges, means you'll have to use a fast-sinking line. But there are times when casting a floating line and a popper can make for adrenaline-pumping action. In either case, casting accuracy is a requirement. Certain spots will produce much better than others and just any cast in the general area will not necessarily draw a strike. For example, wherever large rocks stick out of the water twenty to thirty yards from shore, try to place the fly as close to the rocks as possible. When fishing tidal rips, it pays to cast into the most visible turbulence.

Since cabrilla favor rocky habitat, you have to resign yourself to coming up empty-handed pretty often. For their size, they are very strong and even a three-pound specimen can deliver a hand-wrenching strike when it tries to make off with your fly. Cabrilla do not make the long, sustained runs characteristic of some open-water species, but when you hook one you have to really lean on him to turn him from his rocky lair.

Good cabrilla fishing can be had at the Midriff Islands practically all year long, but the best months seem to be April through November. When the water temperature heats up in the late summer and early fall, you can experience some terrific surface action. The best time for this is early morning and late afternoon, just before dark.

The term *pargo* is the Spanish designation for a variety of snappers, but the one usually sought by anglers traveling to Baja and Central America is the dog (Pacific) snapper. Cabrilla are tough customers, but the pargo is simply one bad critter. More times than I care to admit, these fish have beaten me even on 40- and 50-pound-test class conventional gear. Just imagine how quickly they can humble you on fly tackle.

You face essentially the same set of conditions with cabrilla, but the situation is worse with pargo because they're stronger and generally larger. They are short-yardage specialists, and a brief run is generally all it takes for them to win their freedom. Their broad flanks and broom-wide tails afford them incredible pulling power and it is under-gunned fly fishermen who experience this most directly. In an effort to land some of these brutes, I've resorted to tactics like eliminating the class tippet and going to straight 40-pound mono with a 100-pound shock leader. Don't even think about using the reel; I have worn a water-skiing glove on my stripping hand and still had difficulty trying to hold back line. Once, using a trick passed on to me by Lefty Kreh, I was able to wrap the line around the reel, but the bull of a fish broke the 40-pound leader. My best on the fly rod so far is only an eight-pounder.

Jacks

If you're a poker player you are no doubt familiar with the phrase, "jacks or better." If you're a fly fisherman who has spent any time in warm-water oceans, you also know that when it comes to all-around fun, jacks are better than most. I'm referring to the jack crevalle, of course. This fish is in the same family as the yellowtail, and while the fighting qualities of the latter are superb, the jack rates as an even stronger adversary.

Like yellowtail, jacks can be found both inshore and offshore, but most often you'll find them where shallow and deeper water converge; along reefs, in coves, and along open stretches of beach. When they're chasing bait such as small sardinas they are often within easy casting range of shore-bound anglers. On two occasions I was actually scared out of the water when jacks moved in to mop up bait practically where I was standing. The first time was on the east coast of Costa Rica, where I was fishing out of Bill Barnes' beautiful lodge, Casa Mar. Sharks often cruise very close to the beach, and even though I was only in shin-deep water that's what crossed my mind first when a swirl about the size of a manhole cover erupted about twenty feet from where I was standing. If there was an Olympic medal for the backstep, I would have won it. The second time was on a stretch of beach in Baja. Again, I almost fell over myself trying to get out of the water when the surface exploded in front of me. A few seconds later I was able to determine (from a safe distance up on the beach) that the commotion was being made by rampaging jacks chasing bait. Outside of roosterfish, I can't think of a more sporting fish to take off the beach, and you stand a much better chance of tying into jacks from shore than you do roosters.

The Mexicans call them toro, the Spanish word for bull, and I'm not sure whether this refers to their powerfully-built, compressed bodies, or their fighting qualities. If you have never caught jacks before, about the only disappointment that may register is in relation to their size. They always seem to fight like fish that you would figure to be twice as large. Normally I do not make it a practice to use one of my cus-

Jack crevalle. *Photo by the author.*

tom-crafted fly reels in the surf, but when I think there's a chance of getting into roosters or jacks I definitely take one along.

When hunting toro from a boat, the best time to look for cruising schools is early in the morning when the water tends to be calmest. Bird activity, busting bait, surface swirls and boils, and "nervous water" are the signs to look for. Once you locate jacks, getting them to strike generally isn't much of a problem. I remember Lefty telling me once that he never encountered a jack that wasn't hungry.

Like dorado, jacks are one of the few species that offer consistent top-water action. Whenever possible, I like to fish for them with poppers or the Jungle Jester slider. However, just running across a large school doesn't necessarily mean you will immediately draw strikes. Sometimes they will refuse everything you throw at them. Then you may encounter a second group in practically the same area and you'll find takers. When the fish show initial interest but fail to commit, there are some techniques that may work to change their minds.

One is to speed up the retrieve. This is easier to do with a slider pattern like the Jester because its streamlined head creates less resistance in the water. Sometimes you can do the trick by allowing the bug to pause after a series of rapid strips; a jack will often hit it a moment or two after it sits motionless in the water. Another trick that the late Harry Kime showed me is to make a long strip with your line hand while simultaneously sweeping the rod sideways. You can't get the fly to travel more than several feet doing this, but the accelerated speed often triggers a jack's striking instincts. Obviously, because of their streamlined shape and the fact that they travel through the water, not on top of it, this technique is much better suited to streamers than to poppers.

Jacks have fairly good-sized mouths, so flies and poppers can be tied on hooks ranging from 1/0 to 5/0. They can be such aggressive feeders that I haven't singled out a particular pattern or color combination that produces significantly better than others. When not using poppers or sliders, most of my presentations have been with slightly modified Deceivers. Where jacks are concerned, you can make a fly more attractive by adding more flash in the form of Mylar strips along the sides. The original pattern has worked well, but I have experienced fewer refusals when the fly was dressed more heavily with Mylar.

Sierra

Gaudy Deceivers tied on smaller hooks (sizes 1, 2, and 1/0) will also work wonders with the speedster of the shoreline, the sierra mackerel (*Scomberomorus sierra*). I remember when I first ran into a school tearing up baitfish on a deserted stretch of beach near Loreto in Baja. It was late May and the water temperature hadn't hit its summertime peak. The cooler water, along with an abundance of small sardinas, accounted for the fact that there were still plenty of sierra in the area. I had a small car-top skiff at the time, and I wasn't a hundred yards from the shore when I saw the silvery sardinas shooting out of the water like dimes being sprayed from a giant slot machine.

In four casts I had four successive hookups but never saw a fish. Each time all I brought in was a tippet sans fly. It took that long before I realized that whatever was out there sported scalpel-sharp dentures and if I didn't want to keep donating flies, I had better tie on a short trace of wire. Because these fish tend to run small, you should use light wire. Orvis Super-Flex in 24-pound-test is a good choice. If you use single-strand wire, instead of tying it to the class tippet with an Albright Knot, I find it more convenient to use a small No. 10 black swivel. Connect this to the wire with a Haywire Twist and then tie the tippet to the swivel. This makes for easy changes (all you have to do is cut the tippet at the swivel) and the small swivel doesn't create any more casting problems than the wire. Make sure the swivel is matte black—sierra, needlefish, and wahoo will hit a bright swivel and cut your leader.

Almost an hour went by before I hit another school, but this time I was able to land my quarry. I was also very careful to remove the fly with a pair of duck-bill pliers. For a fish that only went about three and a half pounds, it fought like a turbo-charged bonito. Sierra will get up to ten pounds but most seem to be in the two-and-a-half to four-pound range. But regardless of size, their strike is one of those hand-jolting experiences that keeps you coming back for more. This is a great little gamefish.

Possessed with blurring speed in the water, the sierra is one fish for which it seems you can't strip fast enough. When you combine an accelerated stripping action and the ferocity with which sierra take a fly, you can imagine the force that is exerted against your stripping hand. And once on, a sierra's erratic, zig-zagging antics can make the frantic running of a confused high-school halfback seem relaxed. Although I've caught most of my sierra from skiffs because it's easier to follow rampaging schools, their preference for shoreline habitat makes them a good prospect for those who like to have their feet planted on land. They travel both in schools and singly and are available somewhere in the Sea of Cortez practically year-round. But when temperatures soar during the summer, there are areas around the Cape where they make themselves scarce. Some of the prime months are February through early May.

5

Offshore Fly Fishing

T HE DISTINCTION between inshore and offshore fishing is somewhat arbitrary because many species frequent both zones. At least we don't have to limit ourselves to a definition provided by a weatherbeaten old surf fisherman who once designated "offshore" as any spot that was over his head. The terms "blue water" and "open water" can also be misleading. So instead of trying to establish identifiable demarcation parameters, I'll just concentrate on some of the species that are normally found at least a few miles from shore.

Obviously, the lineup is by no means exhaustive because the discussion will focus only on those species that are within practical range of the fly rodder. For example, on both coasts swordfish are occasionally taken within twenty or so miles of shore on rod and reel but the feat is not all that common even with live bait. The fish are also usually well over one hundred pounds and given their tremendous fighting ability— which is considerably greater than that of marlin—the probability of landing one on anything that could be considered standard fly tackle, let alone inducing a strike on fly, is remote.

The term "standard fly tackle" needs some clarification. I am not a purist and I do not concern myself exclusively with pursuing IGFA records. There are times when I have used class tippets well in excess of the maximum 20-pound test recognized by the IGFA. But the rod-and-reel combinations still conform to the standards established by that organization. One has to draw the line somewhere and, like it or not, after considerable thought and input, the IGFA has done so. Thus, if one were to fish with, say, a five-foot stick like the ones used for big-game, standup style, live-bait fishing, despite the fact that a fly is attached to the line, it would not be considered fly fishing according to the accepted parameters. You could do the same thing at the other end of the scale, using a ten- or 12-foot calcutta stick like the ones used by commercial jackpolers. Here a short length of stout cord is wrapped around the end of the pole and a barbless feathered jig is tied to the tag end of the line. First, the tuna are brought to a frenzy with live chum; then the jig is lowered a few feet below the surface and swished in a sort of S-like pattern. When a tuna strikes it is literally yanked from the water and bounced on deck. Since every fish represents money, the process is repeated over and over again until the school is either depleted or moves on. As a youngster I did this one summer on an albacore boat and loved it. If the tuna fleet were still using this method instead of nets, there would be a lot more fish and they wouldn't kill any porpoise.

There is no reason why you couldn't do the same thing, except with a big winch-like reel like some of the Australians use for bottom fishing. A heavy line could also be cast from one of these calcutta sticks and there is no doubt that you would catch fish. This might be fun, but I would not classify it as fly fishing.

READING THE SIGNS OF THE SEA

WHEN THEY FIRST BEGIN to fish out at sea, many people feel lost (literally and figuratively) and frustrated because they see nothing recognizable. Obviously, this is not how it should be. As one veteran commercial tuna fisherman told me, "Out here it's the eyeballs that count." Modern electronics and navigational devices are vitally important, but for fishing they can only take you so far. If you want to find fish you have to look for them. That's why even the most modern seiners, with all their Space Age electronics, have crew members taking their time-honored watches in the crow's nest, binoculars in hand. The trick to all this, of course, is knowing what to look for. Think of the old salt once again—BBs, birds and bait. Aside from the fish themselves, always be alert for these two significant signs.

The maxim of the sea is that life form follows life form and so it is with birds and bait. The former often indicate the presence of the latter and naturally where there is bait, you can almost always expect larger, predatory gamefish. But before you can look for anything at sea two basic items are absolutely essential—polarized sunglasses and binoculars.

In Chapter 4 we took up the subject of polarized eye wear. As a fly fisherman, for safety, regardless of whether you need them to improve your vision, it's good practice to always wear glasses when chucking flies. I never go anywhere on the water without at least one pair. For offshore use I like the same brown shade that I use for fishing the flats. Brown is not in the same spectrum of colors found in the ocean and thus affords good contrast for spotting fish.

While some people pay little attention to eye wear, far more totally neglect binoculars. If you have fished many of the world's tropical and semi-developed areas, I'm sure you can point to instances where native guides often without benefit of either sunglasses or binoculars demonstrated an uncanny ability to spot fish. Don't draw a false conclusion from this. Their ability comes from years of experience on the water. Imagine how much more proficient they would be with the aid of these two additional items. If you are serious about fishing offshore and either cannot or choose not to rely solely on the services of a professional skipper and crew, you significantly handicap yourself by not using binoculars. If nature had intended us to be predators at sea she would have equipped us with eyes better suited for distance vision. Binoculars provide that necessary option. The higher off the water, the better the view, but even foregoing a tuna tower, your ability to detect birds, bait, flotsam, and minute variations in water-surface movements is greatly enhanced with a pair of binoculars. Under the right conditions it's possible to see for miles.

Just as with your fishing gear, one pair is not necessarily as good as the next, so get the type that is best suited for use out on the ocean. For years, standard naval issue for those who drew deck watches were binoculars with the designation 7x50. The first number (7) refers to the number of times an image is magnified. And contrary to popular misconception, this may not necessarily be associated with the size of the binoculars. Instead, it's more a function of the shape and positioning of the inside lenses. The "50" designation denotes the diameter of the front lens. Called "the objective," this may be likened to the eye's iris in that it controls the availability of light to the eyepiece. The Navy knew its business when selecting 7x50s because they were found to be the most practical combination for ocean-going conditions. Standing on solid ground, a pair with a larger magnification might seem the better choice, but when you're aboard a pitching deck, or perched on a swaying tuna tower, it's entirely different. Any increased magnification will make it more difficult to spot stationary objects so it's best to stick with the 7x50s like the Marine Binoculars made by Minolta. Available through Orvis, these high-quality binoculars have a 372-foot field of view at 1,000 yards and they are waterproof to $3^1/4$ feet for five minutes.

If you want to be successful on the offshore grounds, you must know your birds. For fishing purposes there are five principal varieties that you should pay attention to: frigates, terns, jaegers, sea gulls, and pelicans.

The frigate, or Man-O-War, holds special significance for me because it was one of these high-altitude specialists that led me and Bill Barnes to a school of tuna where I hooked my largest yellowfin on fly. The scene took place on the northeast coast of Costa Rica, about five miles beyond the mouth of the Rio Colorado River. The sea was exceptionally calm and Bill wanted to do a little exploring outside. Neither of us had binoculars because our foray was totally unplanned but we both looked for any possible signs of life. Bill spotted a high-flying frigate on the horizon. As we got closer, the bird circled lower, which meant that bait was near the surface. We were still a good distance off but when the frigate skimmed the surface Bill opened the throttle to get to the area as quickly as possible. The frigate is not a water bird so it can't dive into or land on the surface. Instead, it will pick off surface bait with a graceful sweep of its buzzard-like beak. When the bird made that pass it was a sure sign that bait was being pushed to the surface.

Interestingly, there weren't any other birds in the area but as we got closer we could plainly see surface breaks. Bill shut down the outboard and the small skiff slid to the edge of a scene that neither one of us will ever forget. There were surface-breaking yellowfin everywhere and we were the only ones in the area. Some of the bait apparently sought refuge under the boat, but to no avail, as wine-barrel-bodied tuna picked them off only a few feet below us. As I picked up the fly rod my knees felt like they were filled with Jello. Bill grabbed the only other outfit in the boat, a heavy baitcaster that he used to troll for snook. I don't even remember what lure he tied on, but a fish took it immediately and Bill was spooled in seconds.

I had on a bulky, white Whistler pattern intended for tarpon in the murky river but these yellowfin were in a feeding frenzy, mopping up everything; it only took two strips before I was on to what was at least an eighty- to ninety-pound tuna. We both saw it take the fly and when I struck back it actually paused a second or two before freight-training into the depths. As line began to disappear form the tarpon-size reel, we commented to each other that it wouldn't be long before I too got spooled. But for some reason the yellowfin stopped sounding when I probably had no more than thirty feet of backing left—you could see the spool's arbor. What we thought would be a matter of minutes turned into hours—four to be exact. Gaining only inches at a time, I heard that sickening snap that all fishermen dread because it signals the fact that your line has parted. In this case it was the thirty-pound Dacron. The weak link in the system was the 16-pound-test class tippet, but apparently the Dacron (and it was new) had a bad spot and I lost the contest. But if it weren't for the frigate, the game would never have been played in the first place.

With their somewhat squab-shaped bodies, terns are much smaller than frigates. They can also stay aloft for quite some time. But unlike frigates, with their bomber-scale wing spans, terns continually have to beat their narrow wings with hummingbird-like speed in order to hover above the water. The jaegers are sometimes referred to as "hawks," perhaps because they share a penchant for relative solitude. Like the terns, they often follow the feeding path of marlin and tuna. Sea gulls are probably the best known of all; but because they are confirmed scavengers, they are the least reliable when you're looking for signs of fish. You might see a flock strafing the surface only to find that they are feeding on garbage. They do bear watching, though.

Few people have difficulty identifying the pelican, with its wheelbarrow-proportioned lower jaw. But one thing you may not realize is that this inflatable appendage makes them very adept at scooping up tightly packed pods of bait (called "meatballs," because of the way baitfish group together when chased by larger predators). So when pelicans hit the water it's a good indication that baitfish are in the area.

In many of the world's oceans the primary baits are anchovies, mackerel, squid, sardines, sauries, and flying fish. Larger gamefish like billfish, giant yellowfin, and sharks will also eat smaller gamefish like bonito, skipjack, and juvenile dorado, but for fly-tying purposes you need only concern yourself with the aforementioned baits (flying fish ex-

Action around a kelp paddy. Birds are always a reliable sign of feeding fish. *Photo by the author.*

cepted). Aside from bird action, the principal way to find bait is to see them on the surface. Look for any kind of unusual surface disturbance. Ripples or small wavelets—sometimes called "nervous water"— are usually signs of baitfish swimming on the surface. Periods of slack tide, where there is minimal water movement, are among the best times to look for these signs. Splashes and swirls usually indicate that larger bait like mackerel are in the area. If you have access to a tuna tower you can sometimes spot color patches, which may be schools of baitfish below. You definitely need polarized glasses here.

Baitfish also behave differently when they are being chased. Anchovies and mackerel will ball up, but sauries will frequently spray out of the water like tiny sheets of silver. For those times when nothing is showing on the surface, a good depth sounder becomes a valuable piece of equipment. Even if the bait are beyond the practical range of fly fishing it may be worthwhile to remain in the area because there is always the chance they could be driven nearer the surface by gamefish on the feed.

Breaks in the water current, which often look like miniature oil slicks, also indicate that there is an accompanying temperature change. Tuna are known to frequent the edges where these changes occur. Previously I mentioned the importance of kelp paddies, but any sort of floating structure on the offshore grounds—a log, a piece of cardboard, or a dead sea mammal (perhaps a whale)—can attract bait and accompanying gamefish. Without a good pair of binoculars, much of this could be missed. The ocean is full of life; but you have to learn what to look for.

SHARKS

SHARKS HOLD A STRANGE fascination for fishermen and nonfishers alike. Depending on where you fish for them, they are known by a variety of colorful and often very descriptive names—"grinners," "smileys," "jaws," (this was used long before the book), "the boys in the blue suits," and, as a Costa Rican guide referred to them, the "police." This latter term originated from the manner in which the aggressive bull shark, which frequents those waters, is able to bring an abrupt end to the battle you're having with a gamefish.

For many people, the word "shark" conjures up bad connotations, but as more and more scientific data is accumulated we're finding out that much misinformation is mixed in with some plain old myth. Still, sharks *are* dangerous and they should be handled with great caution and respect; the bottom line is that they are the only gamefish that, given the right circumstances, can and will eat you.

Frankly, this is one of the qualities that first drew me to shark fishing more than thirty years ago. Some of my early outings were off Montauk, New York. The Gulf Stream swings fairly close to the tip of Long Island and during mid-summer and early fall there is a good offshore fishery with a stellar lineup of sharks featuring the likes of blues, tigers, great whites, and last, but far from least, makos. My outings off Montauk were confined to baitfishing; we used mostly chunked bait that was presented in a chum slick consisting largely of heavy-oil-content fish like menhaden, which was ground into a pulverized soup and ladled out as the boat drifted. I didn't realize it then, but this was similar to the technique I was introduced to when I moved back to California in the early 1970s. West Coast fly fishermen from the Bay Area, like the late Myron Gregory, Bob Edgely, and Lawrence Summers, perfected a technique whereby open-ocean sharks like blues and makos could be attracted within range and aroused to the point where they would take a fly.

Prior to their efforts, I don't know of anyone who seriously pursued sharks on the West Coast with fly gear. At the time, most fly fishing for sharks was centered on the shallow flats around the Florida Keys. I sampled some of this myself back then and found wading the shin-deep flats casting flies to blacktip and lemon sharks a very challenging proposition. But the best flats fishing for sharks I ever experienced was at Christmas Island. Most anglers go there for the famous bonefishing and, to a lesser extent, for trevally. But there is also an abundant population of blacktips that seems much more eager to take a fly than their Florida counterparts. Most are small, between three and six pounds. Nevertheless, they're a lot of fun on an 8-weight outfit. But in the continental United States, outside of the Florida Keys, shark fishing is primarily an offshore venture.

Of all the offshore species, sharks are among the most accessible targets for fly fishermen. Still, chumming is essential—as it often is with such other pelagic species as tuna. At times, if you've kept a sharp eye for diving birds or water disturbances, it's possible to pull up on a school of surface-feeding tuna; but even in these cases some type of chum, often in the form of live bait like anchovies, is generally necessary to draw the tuna within range and get them excited to the point where they will take a fly. In some areas it's not uncommon to see blue sharks finning on the surface or a thresher stunning a school of mackerel with broad strokes of its sweeping tail fin. But even under circumstances like these, it would be unlikely to expect any action simply by presenting a fly. Their predatory nature notwithstanding, more often than not, when using artificials for sharks, you will find it necessary to pique their interest by using some form of chum.

One of the attractions of going after sharks is that it is still a relatively uncrowded fishery. For most anglers, whose fishing time may be confined primarily to weekends, this is a definite plus. When popular inshore spots draw boats in numbers that resemble an armada, the offshore grounds often remain almost deserted. When I was running my own boat, many times I would forego a hot bite on inshore species and head offshore just to get away from all the congestion. But this wasn't idle time. When I chummed, I practically never failed to draw sharks to the boat. Often less than fifteen minutes would elapse from the time I hung a chum basket over the side to when the first ominous fin would come slowly but methodically slicing through the surface chop in a sort of stunted zig-zag pattern right for the boat. It's exciting—but it's also eerie.

Following some primitive program put in place by eons of evolution (scientists tell us that sharks have been around for over three million years), sharks like the blue will inevitably home in on the chum basket. On one of my early outings, a good friend, Jerry Pierce, flipped an abomination of a streamer a few feet from the stern and let it hang amidst the bits and pieces of ground chum that were oozing from the basket. The fish came close and I had to shake the basket a few times before I managed to wrench it from its jaws. Then the blue circled off and came in on the chum line again. I was surprised at how gracefully it took the fly along with the chunks of chum. Instead of the wild, thrashing frenzy so often depicted in the movies, blues will frequently glide into the chum slick and almost casually open their jaws to engulf practically anything that looks edible.

Jerry had to strike hard several times before the blue realized it had something strange and mildly annoying lodged in the corner of its jaw. When this sensation registered, the shark coolly headed off for the shipping lanes. Jerry—who had not yet caught a bonito or mackerel on a fly—had on the largest fly-rod fish of his life. He may have been new to fly fishing, but he was an experienced angler and he glanced at me with a look that said: "There's nothing I can do but hang on." The reel was one of those old direct-drive "knuckle busters" and one convincing wrap on his finger was enough to teach him to palm the exposed spool rim while being careful to avoid the whirring handle. The way sound carries over the water I've often wondered if boaters way off on the horizon could hear the noise that reel made when line was tearing out from the spool: it still reminds me of a kid going full speed on a bike, dragging a stick along a picket fence.

Acoustics aside, Jerry hung on and finally was able to turn the shark. Being familiar with light tackle, he had a good idea how much pressure he could apply with the 16-pound-test tippet. But I reminded him during the battle that fighting a shark calls for a different strategy due to the abrasive dentition that covers its body. Shark skin can wear through mono like a high-speed sander, so if the angle is such that the tippet rubs against its body, a wise strategy is to ease up on the pressure. Blue sharks are especially notorious for their twisting and turning tactics and if you follow IGFA regulations and limit yourself to a twelve-inch shock leader (naturally you'll want to use wire) you must resign yourself to the prospect of losing a few fish from time to time. But Jerry was lucky and brought his first blue alongside the boat. Judging by the markers I had spaced along the gunwale, the shark measured roughly 6½ feet, which put it somewhere in the 55- to 65-pound class, a little above average for most specimens in southern California waters. They do not get as large as some of the other sharks but some have been measured as long as thirteen feet.

My personal best was a ten-footer. After five successive tries, I finally was able to bring it to the side of the boat. This bruiser had set up a dining schedule in my chum slick and remained in the area for about two-and-a-half hours. When I first saw it, its pectoral fins looked like the wings on a carrier fighter-jet. From time to time I've hinted to some of my students that they have a flat learning curve. Well, this shark's curve must have dipped. I hooked it on five separate occasions. When it came back in for the sixth time I could actually see two of the flies trailing from the edge of its lower jaw. Obviously, this didn't pose much of a bother because the fish had continued to feed. It ate a sixth fly and this time, because we were about to call it quits for the day, I had Jerry fire up the outboards so we could follow the behemoth blue. In about an hour's time I had him to where we could estimate its length; it was my largest blue ever.

As an aid to pursuing these creatures with fly gear, a few words about their basic physiology and feeding habits are helpful. First, as you may recall from high school biology, the major difference between sharks and other species we commonly fish for is the fact that the shark's skeleton is composed entirely of cartilage. Second, unlike most of the bony fishes, sharks do not have a swim bladder. Their comparatively large and oily liver does add some buoyancy, but by and large sharks have a more difficult time staying afloat than other fishes.

Even their swimming can be a bit problematic because their tails tend to be heterocercal, which is a technical way of saying that the upper fork of the tail fin is larger than the lower. If it were not for their pronounced pectoral fins, their characteristic side-to-side swimming motion could otherwise drive them right to the bottom. Also, to help with the buoyancy and maintain a level attitude in the water, compared to most bony fishes, shark fins are rigid. This is why you'll never see them come to an abrupt stop. If they wish to avoid something, their only course of action is to change course and veer off in another direction. One relevant characteristic for those who fish sharks is their highly developed set of sensory mechanisms. Sight, sound, taste, touch, and smell all function together in the creature's endless quest for food. Their sense of smell is especially acute. Scientists report that sharks can detect something as faint and diluted as one part scent to several million parts water, possibly over a billion parts water.

The feature that draws the most attention is the shark's teeth. On most species they are readily visible and when you're close to them they look like something out of your worst nightmare. Unlike their bony fish counterparts, sharks are covered with a latticework of teeth referred to as denticles. So the skin is actually a continuation of their teeth, and that's why wire is an absolute must. It also explains why a short, twelve-inch leader is such a handicap.

The teeth in bony fishes are set in the jaws, but in sharks they are in the gums. During a frenzied feeding spree some teeth will inevitably break free, but the loss is only temporary because they are equipped with layered rows; this allows ready replacement. One marine biologist reported that in the young of a common species the teeth in the upper jaw were replenished every seven days, while those in the lower jaw were replaced every eight days.

Not only are sharks well equipped, but they also make the most of what they have. For example, blues have so many teeth in the upper jaw that their bases overlap. Their teeth are primarily designed for cutting as evidenced by their triangular shape and serrated edges. From an engineering standpoint, the jaws are pure efficiency. On most species they are hinged in such a fashion that they can be opened to a nearly vertical gape. As the jaws open, the teeth protrude forward; when closing, they tip backward. This means that when they take a bite, it's usually a big one and when they clamp down it's with viselike precision. Even more impressive is the crushing force. One scientist measured the closing force of the jaws of an eight-foot shark and recorded it at an incredible 6,613.8 pounds per square centimeter.

Sharks may have been around millions of years but their sleek, drag-efficient body shape is strictly Space Age. The blue has one of the most streamlined bodies that nature ever graced with fins; this accounts for the fact that, for a given length, the blue weighs less than some other sharks. A seven-footer will weigh in at about seventy pounds, while a nine-footer might tip the scales at about 150 pounds or so. But regardless of size, the feeding habits of blues make them fairly easy game for fly fishermen. Virtually all flesh-eating sharks will scavenge, but numerous field studies have shown that when given a choice, they have a decided preference for fresh meat. This is also the case with blues, though they are less discriminating than some of their close cousins. Records indicate that they will seldom attack large, living creatures, but they sure can get worked up when there's a lot of cutting and slicing going on. For example, when whaling was in its heyday, the frenzied presence of blues during the butchering process was so common that this shark came to be know as the "blue whaler."

Taking a cue from these feeding patterns, with slight modifications, fly fishermen can easily attract blues to a drifting boat and entice them into striking flies. The use of a chum slick, long a common technique on the East Coast, has only recently begun to catch on in California. Traditionally, when West Coast anglers speak of chumming, what usually comes to mind is the practice of tossing out live anchovies. For sharks, however, it is not necessary to go through the trouble of maintaining live bait. Instead, you want to obtain quantities of fresh dead fish with a high oil content, like anchovies, bonito, or mackerel. This will have to be ground up. A hand meat grinder will get the job done but a commercial grinder will make the task much easier. The next step, and this I learned from Bob Edgely and Larry Summers, is to freeze the contents in half-gallon milk cartons. These will store nicely for months at a time. How long you plan to be out will dictate how many cartons you should take on any given outing; as a general guideline I recommend six cartons for a full day's fishing. If you don't want to go through the bother (it can be a messy job) you can buy ground chum from many tackle shops on both coasts.

Once you arrive at the fishing grounds, and depending upon the particular location this may only be a few miles offshore, rip open one of the cartons and put the frozen block into a wire mesh basket that will hang over the side of the boat. Suspend it in such a way that the basket will bob in and out of the water with the motion of the swells. This helps dispense the chum as it begins to thaw and pieces break free from the frozen block. When I first started doing this I used gunny sacks to put the chum in but I soon found that this wasn't a good choice because the ravenous sharks would come right to the source and tear the sack to shreds. You can go through a lot of chum that way—so I now use a more substantial container.

A well-designed setup for dispensing chum is a hard-plastic cylinder from Braid Products called the Chum Mate. It has four big suction cups that make it easy to attach to the side of a boat. A plunger is provided, with stainless steel cutting blades, and when this is used in conjunction with the cylinder suspended over the side of the boat, most of the mess is eliminated. With this system you can use either pre-ground-up chum or you can chop up larger portions with the plunger right out on the fishing grounds. Just be sure to position the cylinder so that the holes in the base and along the sides will bob below the water line, allowing the chum to ooze out. Bits and pieces flake off and are carried away in the drift, creating a delectable trail of tidbits that will eventually attract any sharks in the area. And something that many West Coast anglers are still not apprised of is the fact that the resulting oily slick will attract other predators as well. Mako and thresher sharks (to my knowledge the latter have yet to be taken on fly) and other gamefish like bonito, skipjack, and yellowfin have also been drawn within fly-casting range of the boat. Occasional tugs on the rope attached to a wire basket bobbing in the water will cause greater quantities of chum to ooze out and sometimes this can help bring fish in. But bear in mind that what was true for anchovies is equally applicable here. The function of chum is to attract sharks, not feed them, so it isn't necessary to ladle out huge quantities repeatedly. This will only deplete your supply of chum. Instead, it is more important to maintain a steady, *continuous* chum line. If the slick is broken up, sharks and other predators may not be able to home in on the source.

A common mistake is to become impatient and fail to wait out the slick's attractive potential. If you constantly move to different locations, you generally accomplish little more than wasting valuable chum with nothing to show for your efforts. At times it may be necessary to wait at least an hour before spotting a single shark, but patience generally pays off. When one is sighted, you can be pretty sure that others aren't far away and that it's only a matter of time before they're drawn to the slick. Remember, they have an ability to detect scents that is beyond our comprehension. If one picks up the scent, others will too; having only one shark swimming near the chum line is the exception, not the rule. The largest number I ever counted is sixteen. They were so abundant that they drew the attention of a large sportfisher that was on its way home from Catalina. The skipper was in the tuna tower and he easily spotted what he later said was the largest assembly of sharks he had ever seen outside of an aquarium. This fellow was obviously experienced on the fishing grounds because he shut his engines down and avoided running through the slick. He watched the action for almost two hours before heading back in. I thanked him for his courtesy and his parting comment was something to the effect of "I've got to try that."

While blue sharks can be a lot of fun, makos multiply the excitement several times over. They are not as plentiful as blues, especially since their fine meat has come to be increasingly recognized by a seafood-hungry public, but as a gamefish they have all the requisite qualities. Not only are they real line burners, but along with billfish, dorado, and, to a limited extent, thresher sharks, you can count on some airborne antics when you hook one.

There is usually no mistaking them once they move in on the chum. By comparison, blues seem almost lethargic. The mako, or bonito shark as it's sometimes called, comes into the chum with a kind of steadfast purpose that can make you feel a tad uneasy. Nature designed these blunted beauties as high-speed killing machines and they are outfitted with all the necessary options. Their bulbous shape reminds me of those squat, flared-out Can Am racing cars that are built for running near red-line for long distances. Their teeth resemble curved daggers. They're intended to puncture and hold prey prior to swallowing. But with all this, do not be misled into thinking that they are indiscriminate feeders, because they definitely are not. Blues can seem gluttonous

A Mako shark. *Photo by the author.*

by comparison. It might be analogous to the response you would get by trying to entice a kid to eat a plate of vegetables rather than a dish of ice cream. With makos you will probably find it necessary to alter your tactics slightly.

When I had my skiff at King Harbor, before heading out for sharks I would try to supplement the frozen chum with fresh-caught bonito or mackerel. King Harbor is a great place to fish for both species, and if I wasn't in too much of a hurry, I would use fly gear for this purpose. This was like having and eating your proverbial cake. Bonito are one of the world's great gamefish and you couldn't ask for a better day than when you started off catching them on fly gear, only to use some of them later as enticements for even bigger game that you would challenge on similar tackle.

Marlin fishermen from time to time make incidental catches of makos when the latter attack their trolling lures. However, for fly fishermen at least, it is best to go with the chumming technique just described. If they are in the area, ground-up chum will attract makos but it may not be sufficient to entice them into striking the fly. (Blues can also get finicky, so what I'm about to relate may also apply to them.) If the fly is laying back in the slick and is not being picked up even after you have imparted such different actions as twitching it a few times or retrieving it a short distance, you might give the following a try. Strip the fly from the water and begin to throw intermittent chunks of fresh bonito or mackerel into the water. These pieces can be about 1 to 1½ inches square, the fresher the better. Throw them hard, so there is a definite splash when they hit the water. Allow the shark to pick one off, then wait several seconds and toss in another piece. Repeat this four or five times or until you feel the shark is beginning to get into a pattern. Then, with the shark in casting range, after the last piece has been thrown, slap the fly hard on the surface. I have taken many makos on a fly, and most have responded to this technique. It's an exciting way to fish because everything is so visual—and you have the added satisfaction of having deceived this cunning hunter.

The first one I took in this manner was in the shipping lanes approximately half way to Catalina Island. A number of blues were in the slick, when my friend Pete Wight (I called him "great white" after this) spotted a mako heading for the chum. It made a couple of turns at my white fly, which I had heavily adorned with strips of silver Mylar to add flash, but it wasn't interested enough to eat the fly. That's when I had Pete start throwing chunks of mackerel. We didn't have much to throw out so Pete only did this three or four times. When I slapped the fly down after the last chunk was thrown, the aroused mako went for it just like it was another piece of mackerel. I waited for him to turn to make sure he had it and then I struck back on the line. It moved out about as fast as anything I've ever had on the end of my line and then came shooting out of the water, creating a scene I'll never forget. I've had fish like tarpon and sailfish make some spectacular jumps, but perhaps because this was my first mako or perhaps because all this great action took place just a few miles from home, this particular leap always stands out in my mind. When I weighed it back at the dock, it only went forty-five pounds, but the fish's jaws are sitting right beside my desk as a constant reminder of what great gamefish makos are.

A second alternative is to tease the fish in by using a live bait like a mackerel tethered on a hookless line. The person manning this teaser rig will have to be alert because a mako can devour the fish with lightning speed. The trick is to try to pull the mackerel away from the shark several times—although if it does eat the live bait immediately, it will usually want another. You don't want to keep feeding the fish because it could lose interest and move on. Usually the live offering really excites the shark and if you can quickly get a fly in front of it when the mackerel is pulled away, the shark will go for it with a vengeance.

I was using a 12-weight outfit that I consider standard for this type of fishing. Because of this particular fish's size, I could have landed it on a 9- or 10-weight, but when you get into larger sharks, you'll need the heavier outfit, especially in the final phase of the battle where you must pump the fish up from the depths. Casting distance isn't a factor so you do not have to use full-length lines; besides, with a shortened line, you can get more backing onto the reel and have less line-drag to contend with when the shark is a long distance from the boat. Floating lines work best but there are times when the sharks are a little deeper, at which times you might opt for an intermediate or slow-sinking line.

For shark fishing, fancy, artistic creations aren't needed. When someone asked the late Myron Gregory what flies he used for sharks, I heard him give the following explanation: "Take a vacuum cleaner and vacuum the area around your fly-tying desk. Then empty the bag, take a fistful of whatever was sucked up and tie this to the hook shank." He was exaggerating but his point was, you don't need elaborate patterns for flies that will be drifting in a chum slick. Bulk is probably the most important consideration. The fly's silhouette should roughly conform to the chunks of chum you are using. Four to eight neck hackles, two to four inches in length, tied with the curved ends splayed out, offer a good simulation of pieces of ground-up chum. Blood leeches out quickly so most bits and pieces look white after only a few minutes in the water. Most of my flies are tied accordingly.

Opinion is divided concerning what to do with a shark once you have it boatside. The decision should be a simple one. Just as with all gamefish, if you do not wish to eat it, it should be released in as prime condition as possible. Fly fishermen have earned the reputation of being more conservation-minded than most other anglers and I hope that this will be so even for sharks. They play a vital role in the ocean's ecological system and the practice of indiscriminately killing them is unwarranted. The safest way to release a shark—for both parties—is simply to cut the leader. Flies will not cause any real damage; the hook will quickly dislodge or rust out.

Bringing a shark on board can be a dangerous undertaking and is best left to experienced hands. On one trip back to port I had a sixty-pound mako that was destined for the dinner table stretched out across my stern. The fish had been gutted and was apparently dead. About twenty minutes underway, the outboards began to sputter and then they completely quit. I turned to address the problem and saw that the mako had chewed through the fuel line. Don't take *anything* for granted when you're dealing with sharks.

TUNAS

TUNA ARE SOME OF the most magnificent creatures in the sea, beautifully programmed by nature with a genetic script that has been finely tuned through aeons of evolutionary development. They don't have to spend time improving their bodies because from the day they're born they function at absolute maximum. Given the reality of their environment with the age-old division between predator and prey, anything less would spell imminent death. Their lives have a simple elegance. There is no time for leisure or rest. Instead, they engage in an endless quest for food interrupted by only brief periods for reproduction to ensure the survival of the species.

Since they are members of the same family, much of what I had to say regarding bonito holds true for albacore, bluefin, bigeye, skipjack, and yellowfin.

Of all the tunas, the availability of albacore is the most difficult to predict. On the West Coast, at least, two principal factors play a key role in determining whether or not they will make a showing in any substantial numbers: water temperature (60 to 68 degrees Fahrenheit is considered the ideal range) and the availability of bait, primarily anchovies and sauries. If all goes well, these long-finned, white-meat members of the tuna family generally start showing up off northern Baja sometime in June, usually in the area around Guadalupe Island. If everything is to their liking, they swing within a reasonable distance of the coast on their

Yellowfin Tuna.

northward migration. But even when they do, they normally remain at least thirty to forty miles offshore. If there were ever a "here today, gone tomorrow" type of fish, the albacore would certainly qualify.

If you manage to get into a decent-size school and have plenty of bait, you stand a good chance of getting some great action on the fly. Over the years, I've often claimed that this world-class gamefish is not a particularly difficult fish to catch, at least when you're bait fishing. Of course, this has to be taken in perspective. Finding them can require considerable experience and skill, so if you don't have the services of a professional skipper and are running your own boat, just from the standpoint of safety alone, you'd better know what you are doing. The sea is unforgiving.

This is where the anglers riding the commercial passenger-carrying sport boats have a decided advantage. They have an experienced skipper and crew taking care of everything from navigational chores to chumming. Unfortunately, the conditions on board these boats are generally not conducive to fly fishing. A second significant advantage these bigger boats have is their enormous bait-carrying capacity. Tuna are always hungry and they won't linger long in an area that doesn't promise plenty of food. If you find them and want to hold them for a while, you're going to need a good deal of chum in the form of live anchovies. And this is all the more critical where fly fishing is concerned, because many times you'll need added inducements to get the fish to strike an artificial. Furthermore, albacore will often hang in the depths well beyond the practical range of even fast-sinking lines. They'll come nearer the surface if they detect a food source; to effect this, you'll need to chum. When they're aroused and within range they will normally take a fly readily, but even under these conditions I recommend a fast-sinking line. The current is often strong and albacore, like their other tuna counterparts, take most of their offerings at least a foot or more below the surface.

The flies I have found most productive on tuna are relatively small, sparsely tied patterns. Two patterns I developed especially for members of the tuna family, the Sardina and the Tuna Tonic, have worked well. For albacore in the fifteen- to thirty-pound class, hook sizes can range anywhere from 1/0 to 4/0. Even when used in conjunction with sinking lines, I like the fly to descend quickly. This can prove the "hot ticket" when stripping the fly quickly and then suddenly pausing for a brief moment. The fly will flutter just like stunned or wounded anchovy and anything that represents an easy meal is quickly taken.

Though conditions vary, on the offshore grounds members of the tuna clan seem to respond best when the fly is moving quickly. Even bonito, which often go for a slow to moderate retrieve in the harbors, seem to prefer a fast-moving fly out in the ocean. I'm not sure exactly why, but my guess is that this may have something to do with the way bait behaves in different surroundings. In the relatively close confines of harbors, bait can't run off for long distances; instead, they dart and flutter as they seek cover along jetties, dock walls, mooring buoys, and the like. But in the open ocean they're often chased down on the run and a fly that resembles a baitfish frantically swimming for its life may more readily blend in with the natural order of the environment.

One problem (of course this may not be perceived as such by some anglers) that you may frequently encounter with albacore is that skipjack are often mixed in with them. When this is the case, it will be difficult to get an albie to take a fly because the "skippies" are faster and more aggressive. They simply beat them to the fly. Skipjack are a great gamefish in their own right and I can't say that albacore give a better account of themselves. In fact, if anything, skipjack may even be stronger—though albacore get top billing. This is probably due to the fact that they make excellent table fare. However, if it's great sport you're after, don't thumb your nose at skipjack. They are one of the most exciting fish to see in a chum line as they come through and mop up bait with such incredible speed that you only catch a glimpse of their bullet-shaped bodies glowing a beautiful iridescent blue, looking like a series of flashbulbs going off under water.

Skipjack and yellowfin, especially in Mexican waters, can also be found much closer to shore than albacore. There have even been times when skippies were inside King Harbor. The first time I hooked one on a fly I thought I might have on at least a ten-pound-class bonito. When I first saw the color I still couldn't identify the fish but was surprised because it didn't look that big in the water. When I finally got it boatside, I saw that it was a skipjack and only about five pounds at that. I shudder to think what they could do if they grew to the size of giant yellowfin.

When the latter fish start going over the hundred-pound mark, I think you can pretty much write them off as far as standard fly-fishing gear is concerned. With 20-pound-test tippets and regulation fly rods, the prospect of maneuvering these brutes up out of the depths borders on fantasy. Even their school-size counterparts in the fifteen- to forty-pound class will put you and your tackle through a thoroughly taxing workout. They may not exhibit the aerial acrobatics of dorado, sailfish, or marlin, but in terms of sheer strength and staying power, yellowfin are unmatched.

Yellowfin are worldwide. They range in areas as widely separated as Montauk and the Sea of Cortez. Along with the bird and bait action that signal the presence of gamefish, with yellowfin look also for traveling schools of surface-jumping porpoise. Not only are they fun to watch, but especially in the summer and early fall they serve as key indicators of yellowfin.

Tuna are constantly on the move, so it is often a game of hunt and chase. That's why a relatively small, fast, and highly maneuverable boat can be so effective. The trick is to position yourself well ahead of the porpoise and troll feathers tied on leadheads a fair distance off the stern. Yellowfin seem to prefer trolling lures that are positioned well beyond the wake, often as far as thirty to forty yards back. When one of these lines gets bit, the boat should be put in neutral and the fly cast to the area behind the stern. Again, fast-sinking lines are necessary because the tuna frequently hang below the porpoise. Procuring live bait for chumming isn't always practical so most of the time you don't really have any means of enticing the fish to the surface. This is one situation where patience can pay big dividends. It's tempting to start retrieving the fly as soon as it hits the water but a better course of action is to give it time to get down. There are no precise guidelines here but as a rule I try to wait to a mental count of at least twenty before I begin stripping line. Sometimes I interrupt the retrieve after six or seven fast pulls and allow the line to sink back down again before stripping it in preparation for another cast.

If the porpoise frequently change direction, as they are prone to do, instead of frantically trying to maintain position a good tactic may be simply to stop the boat, cut the engine, and drift. You might get lucky and have the porpoise and the tuna move right in on you. Shutting off the engine is the principal factor in inducing the school to come to the boat. Even on the offshore grounds, when tuna are running boat traffic can get heavy and a frequent mistake that novice and overanxious anglers make in this type of fishing is trying to run their boat right on top of the porpoise. When you see other boats hooked up, avoid running your craft smack in the middle of their area because you'll ruin the bite for everyone. The proper procedure is to hang back a respectable distance and try to position yourself to drift toward the school without running the engines. There have been times when I have drifted with as many as a dozen boats or so within fifty yards of each other with everyone enjoying good action. Where porpoise are involved, you have to bear in mind that even though they are relatively carefree animals and are frequently known to frolic in a boat's wake, they are not going to linger around when they are being intercepted by boats from every direction with their engines roaring. When this happens, the porpoise will keep changing direction, the tuna will sound deeper, and you will end up burning more fuel for fewer fish.

DORADO

IF THERE IS ONE offshore gamefish tailormade for the fly rod it has to be the dorado—otherwise known as the dolphinfish or, in Hawaii, mahi. It is one of the most voracious feeders in the sea and will eat practically anything it can clamp its jaws on. Outside of tarpon and sailfish, I'm hard-pressed to think of a more acrobatic species when hooked and in terms of overall beauty, with their rainbow-like coloration, they swim in a league all their own. These fish roam the world's oceans but thrive in the tropical seas and prefer water temperatures in the 72- to 88-degree Fahrenheit range.

The dorado's almost insatiable appetite makes it a very fast growing species, similar to the tunas in this respect. In one year's time they can put on about ten pounds. A "big moe" in the forty-pound-plus range may only be about four years old. In many areas there are two classes of fish, the "juveniles" (from five to ten pounds) and the "heavyweights" (in the twenty-five-pound-plus category). It's not often that you encounter a fish much over forty pounds.

Regardless of size, all dorado respond well to flies but the juveniles are more reckless than the larger fish; perhaps they get a little wiser with age. In any case, the larger males (they can be distinguished by their high forehead and their solitary nature, which seldom finds them traveling with more than two or three of their kind) sometimes can become

Weedlines, color changes, or flotsam in offshore waters often indicate the presence of dolphin, which are spectacular fighters on the fly rod. *Photo by Mark Sosin.*

selective. Under these circumstances you might try the bait-and-switch technique described in the section on roosterfish. Troll a hookless strip bait like bonito or dorado belly about fifty feet behind the boat. When a fish pops up behind the teaser have one person manipulate the line to get the dorado aroused by giving it a little taste. When the bait is jerked from the water the angler should make the cast and be prepared for action. Ideally, the fly should bear at least a faint resemblance to the teaser, although over the years friends and I have had favorable results on color patterns that included all white, yellow and white, green and yellow, and blue and white. As saltwater fish go, dorado do not have very large mouths so I tie most of the flies on hook sizes ranging from 1s to 3/0s. When using streamers I like to slap the fly down hard on the surface to get the fish's attention. If the fish is sufficiently aroused, you will see it "light up" and it will be in no mood to fool around: the fly is usually pounced on in short order.

Because the dorado is such an habitual surface feeder, you'll find that poppers are effective offerings. The late Harry Kime convinced me of this years ago; following his technique, I still tie many of my bugs with a closed-cell synthetic material resembling Styrofoam known as Ethafoam. The popper bodies for the smaller fish can be about the size used for freshwater bass, about $1^{1}/4$ inches in length with a $^{5}/8$-inch diameter. For larger fish I step things up a bit. A bug with a two-inch body length and $^{7}/8$-inch slanted face can create quite a surface disturbance and this is what it often takes to draw a big dorado's attention. Hooks should also be larger—anywhere from 3/0 to 5/0. These fish do have teeth so by all means use a shock leader; fifty-pound mono affords ample protection. When using strip baits as teasers, I leave most of the popper white because that's what the belly section will look like after being dragged through the water for a while. But color really isn't all that critical in poppers because it is the surface commotion that serves as the principal attraction.

In line with their surface-feeding patterns, dorado, like few other fish in the sea show a penchant for floating objects, be they weedlines or broken cardboard boxes. The rule of thumb when hunting these colorful gamesters is to find the flotsam and you're more than likely to find the dorado. When you do locate them under floating debris it's often possible to get them to strike without the aid of additional attractors. You can bring this off with a popper. Cast the bug to the floating structure, make one or two strips, and then let it sit for a few seconds. If a dorado moves to inspect it but doesn't take, lift the popper off the water and make a second cast to the same spot. Make one or two more pops and then haul it back and cast again. Each time you do this the fish should become more and more excited. When the dorado starts to get that beautiful neon glow, you know you've got him aroused; the next time the popper lands on the water, chances are it won't move too far before the "raging bull" tears into it.

Dorado often follow one of their kind that has been hooked. I have observed this phenomenon with a number of other species, but it is nowhere near as pronounced as with dorado. For this reason, knowledgeable anglers often play a dorado longer than necessary just to attract others to the boat that may be milling about the area. Even if there are only two or three fish in a particular location, if one of them is hooked, the others are almost sure to follow. One time when a friend and I were skimming along a weedline off south Florida, we had a dorado come up behind the teaser that we were trolling on a boat line. It was my turn to cast and when the fish got within range I tossed out a popper; it was taken almost immediately. When the fish was within fifty or so feet of the boat, we could see that two other dorado were closely following it. My friend cast his popper and now he was on too. If there were a third angler on board, I'm sure we would have had a trio of hookups going.

WAHOO

OVER THE YEARS I have used up quite an array of adjectives trying to describe this dynamic member of the king mackerel family. By any standards the wahoo has to rank as one of the wildest fish in the sea. I've logged a good deal of experience with these but most of this has been on long-range trips based out of San Diego; we fished areas down off the Baja peninsula like "the ridge" and the famed Revilaggedo Island chain hundreds of miles south of Cabo San Lucas. Some of the largest concentrations of wahoo and yellowfin you'll ever encounter roam these waters and as far as I can tell, I was the first to fly fish for them on these trips. I made some memorable catches, but to be candid, a lone fly fisherman in the company of twenty-plus other anglers is a distinct disadvantage. Our casting method requires more room than presentations made with

Wahoo. *Photo by the author.*

conventional and spinning tackle so you have to pick a spot where you won't interfere with the other fishermen on board. This usually involves casting from the bow; and to do this you must first clear everything with the skipper. If you do have an opportunity to present the fly (and this may only involve a simple roll cast) there is the chance of hooking into some world-class gamefish. Bear in mind, however, that you do not have the luxury of the boat chasing down the fish for you. When you have to battle large gamefish from a stationary platform in the company of other anglers who are also locked on to fish, light tackle, regardless of the gear, takes on an entirely different perspective.

In January of 1976 (January through March are prime months for wahoo both at the Cape and the islands below), I hooked my largest wahoo ever under this set of conditions. The traditional method of locating these fish is by means of trolling. Strip baits can be used but on long-range trips it's all done with artificials. When one of the trolling lines gets bit, the boat's engines are put into neutral and the vessel will slide some distance before coming to a stop. The instant the skipper or crew member gives the signal, the other anglers begin casting metal jigs or fishing live bait like anchovies, mackerel, or caballito. On this occasion, my friends gave me the chance to cast from the port stern corner when the trolling lines were cleared—and to everyone's amazement, including my own, I got struck after making only four or five strips. In fact, I was one of the few to get bit on that stop. Unfortunately, it was a short-term connection but the memory of it all will remain forever. The seasoned skipper and two crew members who witnessed all this estimated the wahoo to be in the eighty-pound class. When it struck, the few feet of line lying on deck shot up and hissed through the guides like it was being sucked away by a giant vacuum. Then the fish rocketed into the air a good ten feet or so, its magnificent streamlined body silhouetted a mere second or two against the sun-scorched backdrop of Socorro Island. It continued to burn line when it landed and moments later there was that sickening sensation of slack. At first I thought and hoped that the fish had merely changed direction. This is common with wahoo; in this they are rather like their smaller inshore brethren, the sierra.

Everyone shouted, "Reel, reel!" What most of them didn't realize was that the single-action fly reel had only a 1:1 gear ratio. Anyway, it was all for naught and after almost a full minute of winding line it became painfully obvious that the wahoo and I had parted company. Curiously, it was the wire shock leader that had broken; and I was using single-strand twenty-seven-pound test. The only explanation I can venture is that the wire apparently kinked when the fish jumped. This is one drawback to single strand.

For years I dreamed of fly fishing these waters under more opportune conditions and recently this has become a reality as a number of long-range operators have begun offering trips designed exclusively for fly fishermen. Being involved in the Orvis tackle-testing program, I had the honor of participating in the second such long-range trip of its kind, a bluewater fly-rod invitational organized by Ed Rice, president of International Sportsmen Expositions. Frank LoPreste, a pioneer in long-range fishing, ran the first fly-rod outing on the *Royal Polaris*. On this trip we were fortunate to have him join skipper Tim Ekstrom aboard the *Royal Star*.

To maximize everyone's fishing opportunities, these are special limited-party outings. For example, aboard the 92-foot *Royal Star*, we had sixteen top-flight saltwater fly rodders. The boat carried four Avon inflatables and once we arrived at the fishing grounds these were lowered into the water where everyone had a chance to fish from them on a rotational basis. A similar pattern was established for fishing on the mother ship. The stern corners are the most productive areas because this is where the live chum in the form of anchovies, sardines, and mackerel are constantly dispensed from the huge aft bait tank. Live chum is the key to success on these trips and every day the water was alive with yellowfin and skipjack that shot in and out of the stern area taking advantage of the free offerings. While they usually do not travel in large schools like the former, roving wolf packs of wahoo were also attracted by the chum. They also homed in on the smaller skipjack as many of us found when we had nothing but cleanly severed heads hanging on our flies.

The waters off Baja are one of the few places in the world where wahoo do not represent incidental catches. They are so abundant that it is not wishful thinking to set your sights on them; in a seven-day fishing period, fly rodders on the *Royal Star* landed fifteen wahoo.

In fishing wahoo with conventional tackle, if slightly more than fifty percent of the hooked fish are landed, the angler is considered successful. They may not have the all-out staying power of tuna, but wahoo are not easy fish to bring to the boat. Many times you part company the instant the fly is taken. Wire is an absolute must, but following IGFA regulations, you are only allowed twelve inches and often this is simply not long enough to prevent a cutoff. A wahoo's mouth is anything but soft and when you combine this factor with its blinding speed and ability to change direction like erratic lightning bolts, you begin to understand why it's difficult to keep a fly firmly planted in its jaws.

This particular trip, combined with years of pursuing wahoo on standard long-range outings, provided a number of lessons applicable to fly fishing the "wild ones."

For one thing, wahoo like a lot of flash. Consistently, regardless of shape, the metal jigs that have proved most effective on these trips have been chrome. Following this, I would recommend adding strands of silver Mylar or Flashabou to any fly you're tying for wahoo. A particularly successful pattern that incorporates large bunches of Mylar is Ralph Kanz's Bucktail Baitfish. The master fly tyer Dan Byford created another hot pattern he named, appropriately enough, Mylar Madness.

When there is plenty of live chum available, one of the best ways to fish these flies is simply to cast them out and allow them to sink. Ed

Rice first showed me this and I was initially skeptical because it is commonly recognized that wahoo prefer fast-moving offerings. Conventional reels featuring high-speed gear ratios like 5:1 and 6:1 are considered standard when retrieving lures for wahoo. But this, of course, is not an absolute. And with flies, conditions are not the same because hair and feathers behave differently from solid-bodied artificials. I always start with a rapid stripping motion; but I'm always ready to change tactics. Not that many wahoo have been taken on a fly and no rules are yet set in stone. I recall one time off the East Cape region of Baja when a junior-size wahoo about three feet long came by and ate my fly as it sank. Other than its descent in the water, there was no movement, yet the fish still saw fit to eat it. When you consider a wahoo's streaking speed, it's pure fantasy to think that you can strip the fly fast enough to turn them on. Instead, I suspect that a sinking fly resembles an injured baitfish, and despite the wahoo's ability to run down practically anything that swims, like other predators they take advantage of an easy meal whenever the opportunity presents itself.

When fishing from a private boat your best shot at wahoo is by trolling teasers, preferably strip baits like the ones used for dorado and billfish. But wahoo are like roosters in the sense that they will come up for the teaser but not linger long. Since this is the case, speed is of the essence. When you see one flashing behind the teaser, get the boat out of gear and make the cast to the teaser as quickly as possible; wahoo will soon lose interest. Even if you have live bait for chumming, wahoo won't mill around like dorado or tuna.

BILLFISH

THE PROSPECT OF TAKING billfish on fly gear was at one time regarded as pure fantasy. But fortunately every endeavor has its visionaries and the late Wes Robinson is credited with taking the first sailfish on a fly rod in January 1962. Ten years ago most anglers were still awestruck by such a feat, but today, at least with sailfish, it is becoming more and more commonplace. In comparison to other members of the billfish family, sails are relatively easy to tease. Eventually any fish will lose interest but sails tend to be the most responsive in this respect. They also don't get to the behemoth sizes characteristic of marlin so it's possible to handle them on fly gear.

Marlin are another matter. Stripes and a few blacks have been taken on regulation fly tackle, and only recently the Pacific blue has entered the record books. Mike Sakamoto from Hawaii managed to take a 200 pounder in 1989 but the fly was trolled and the leader didn't conform to IGFA specifications. Finally, in February 1991, Tim Gray, fishing thirty-five miles south of Flamingo Bay, Costa Rica, became the first angler to land a Pacific blue on regulation fly tackle. This fish weighed 203 pounds, 8 ounces and on 16-pound tippet that is an outstanding accomplishment. Part of the problem with blacks and blues is finding specimens that are small enough to be fought successfully on fly gear. That was my difficulty two years ago when I hooked what was probably the largest Pacific blue on regulation fly tackle.

This took place out of a great little lodge on the northwest coast of Costa Rica appropriately named Bahia Pez Vela because these are some of the most prolific grounds anywhere for Pacific sails. Bill Barnes and I were trying for the 8-pound tippet record that Billy Pate captured a month later (only to have it broken again by Jim Watt almost a year later). We exhausted our supply of pre-tied leaders and the sail fishing was so hot that every time we started making up new ones, we had to stop what we were doing either to handle one of the teasers or pick up the fly rod, depending on whose turn it was to cast. We still had plenty of 16-pound tippets and since we were running low on flies, we decided to start using the heavier leaders. At about high noon, the action tapered off and I began to snooze in one of the deck chairs. It always amazes me how quickly one awakens when someone yells "Fish." In this case it was our captain shouting, "Pez, pez," and it was only a brief moment before my eyes focused on a huge dorsal fin cutting the surface behind one of the strip baits. Bill grabbed the teaser rod and began trying to draw this enormous creature closer to the boat. However, instead of trying to stimulate the fish's interest, Bill found himself struggling to prevent it from completely devouring the bait. When he fist spotted the dorsal he shouted that it was the largest sail he had ever seen. But our experienced skipper, Nelson, had a better view from the bridge and he knew at once that this was no sailfish. It charged the boat, trying to eat the teaser, on five separate occasions and Bill complained that his arms were getting tired from trying to wrench the bait from the great fish's jaws.

Finally, when Nelson managed to get the boat about forty-five feet from the fish, Bill jerked the teaser, the boat's engine was put into neutral, and I made my cast. Despite the fact that this was the biggest fish I had ever faced with a fly rod, I was able to put the bulky tandem-hook fly where it had to be and the massive form moved on it immediately. The take was text-book perfect. The fly stuck in the soft tissue in the upper corner of the jaw behind the base of the bill. I struck with three quick, short strips and Nelson immediately had the boat tracking the fish so I wouldn't get spooled. The great fish never jumped or sounded and at least a half dozen times we were able to get close enough to hazard a guess as to its size. From the vantage point of the bridge Bill and Nelson estimated that it went between 350 and 400 pounds. At one point when we got alongside it they both agreed that it was about half the length of the 26-foot boat.

I don't know if I ever hurt that fish. I put everything I had into him but with 16-pound test you just do not have any control over something that big and powerful. I would like to think that I tired it a bit but judging from the way it continued to swim I doubt that I did. Bill half jokingly remarked that he wouldn't be surprised if the marlin started feeding. My total fighting time was four and half hours. We were going farther and farther out to sea, fuel was getting low, the seas started to kick up, and it was nearing nightfall. At this point it was either turn him or break him off and in the most difficult move in my lifetime of fishing I clamped down on the spool and severed the connection with one of the sea's most awesome creatures.

In its relatively brief history, pioneers in the sport like the late Wes Robinson, Jim Paddock, Rick Defoe, Billy Pate, Bill Barnes, the late Harry Kime, and Winston Moore, to name a few, have developed a set of well-proven techniques for teasing and fighting billfish on fly gear; a considerable amount of this development has taken place and continues to take place in Baja waters. It is no coincidence that this is where Wes Robinson took the first striped marlin on a fly back in 1965. Sails are around the Cape on nearly a year-round basis, but the area has really become famous for its striped marlin population. Mid-October to February are generally the best months.

Despite the fact that in these fish-rich waters there are times when you can see marlin slashing bait on the surface, it would be relatively fruitless to blind cast to these swordsmen of the sea. Yet, to comply with

IGFA regulations, the fly must be cast, not trolled. The later technique is used only to tease the fish to within casting distance of the angler. The procedure may vary, depending upon the size of the boat and number of crew, but as a general rule three lines are trolled, one from each stern corner and one boat line (this is a handline) from the middle of the transom. The corner lines are trolled on rod-and-reel combinations and for this application I prefer high-speed, conventional saltwater reels (6:1 ratios are a good choice) over spinning tackle. In an offshore environment, conventional reels are less prone to failure and afford better control when manipulating a bait over a choppy surface or when trying to yank it away from a determined billfish. The high-speed ratio is an advantage when you want to get the teaser away as quickly as possible. A 7½- to 8-foot rod with a fairly stiff tip is recommended for handling the strip baits. The teasers will not skip the surface properly with a rod that has a soft action. In addition, when a billfish grabs one of the teasers it often takes a considerable amount of force to pull it away from him so you'll need a rod with backbone to accomplish this without undue delay.

The stern corner lines are usually staggered behind the boat at distances varying from thirty to seventy feet. These are generally the bait lines, often belly strips cut from dorado, bonito, or skipjack. The middle line may incorporate a bird teaser with a daisy chain of plastic skirts or squid. Sometimes a strip bait is attached to the terminal end of this setup. It has been my experience that the strip baits are generally more effective than artificials in arousing the fish's interest. When a billfish gets a taste of the real thing, it often wants more and will keep coming to get it. Artificials can be effective in initially getting the fish's attention, but if the fish latches on to an artificial lure it will reject it more readily than it would a strip bait.

Regardless of what they come after, the sight of the dorsal slicing through the surface and the bill slashing at prey that the fish was deceived into thinking would be an easy meal is one of the most emotionally charged scenes in the world of sportfishing. And this is where the thrill of fly fishing takes on a dimension all its own. In other forms of angling, when the sail or marlin charges the offering, the strike hopefully soon follows and the fish begins its struggle for freedom. With fly gear, however, there is an additional scene to this drama that plays out the excitement to the absolute limit. This unfolds in the process of teasing the fish to a point where it is sufficiently aroused to strike a fly as a substitute offering. The event is so visually stunning that regardless of the role you play, the exhilaration and anticipation experienced can put everyone's emotional circuits on overload.

However, the level of excitement notwithstanding, everyone involved must keep "cool" because a successful outcome demands total teamwork, where timing is everything. The person doing the teasing plays a key role. He must make sure that the fish is sufficiently aroused—and this takes experience. With a strip bait you want to give the fish a taste but not too much. If the fish completely engulfs the bait you may have difficulty getting it back. Or, if it manages to thoroughly mangle it, the fish may no longer chase the food. The object is to get the fish into a mood where it keeps coming back for more. There is a *feel* involved in doing this that is difficult to describe; it involves striking an artful balance between the extremes of being either too generous or too stingy. When a billfish, like so many pelagic species, gets excited it will "light up" in a sort of iridescent blue. Whether it is frustrated, excited, or a combination of the two, no one knows for sure. But you do have its attention.

The person controlling the bait must also make certain the fish is coaxed to within casting range of the angler. Ideally, the teasers should not be jerked away from the fish at a distance farther than the angler can cast the bulky fly. However, there are times when a dropback may be necessary to maintain or rekindle a fish's interest.

Before the process ever begins the angler strips off a length of line he is able to cast. To insure that the coils of line lie properly, the fisherman should make a practice cast or two and then strip the line back in and carefully drop it into a bucket. When the "moment of truth" arrives the last thing you want is a tangle in the running line; adding a little water to the bucket makes the line shoot out easier. Also, pre-wetting the streamer will cause it to sink as soon as it hits the water. You don't want it lying on the surface like a big feather duster after you make the cast.

It is the person manning the teaser who should make the decision as to when the fish is sufficiently aroused and at the appropriate distance from the boat. When this is established, and it generally only takes a matter of seconds, the teaser person will yell something like "Now" and jerk the offering away from the fish. This is when timing is critical. At that instant, the boat is put into neutral and the angler makes his cast. With as little delay as possible, the object is to have the fly substitute for the displaced teaser. If there is too much time lag, the fish may become disinterested and swim away.

Preparation and attention to minute details are the keys to success in this type of fishing. Carefully coiling the pre-determined length of shooting line in a bucket is only one of the precautions against possible line foul-ups. Guided by the law that anything which can possibly snag a fly line will inevitably do so, experienced billfishermen carry large rolls of wide masking tape to cover any protrusions like boat cleats and the like. Even a short fighting butt on a rod or a protruding drag knob on a reel can take their toll.

There are a number of effective rigging procedures used when fly rodding for billfish and what I'm about to discuss is a compilation of information based on both personal experience and what I've learned from some of the top anglers in the sport.

First off, you want the best gear available. Starting with the Dacron backing, some anglers go with 20-pound test because its smaller diameter creates less drag in the water and they can pack more on the spool. I prefer 30-pound test for added insurance especially when using 20-pound-test class tippets. To the backing you can attach a length of 30-pound running line (about fifty feet is all you need), or go directly to a hundred-foot length of high visibility, 30-pound monofilament. Due to its stretch factor, which is practically nil in Dacron, the mono serves as a cushioning agent. A high-visibility line is preferable because this makes it easier for the skipper to monitor so he can run the boat in the appropriate direction, given the fish's position. With a Bimini Loop in both the Dacron and mono, interlocking the two loops creates a strong connection between the lines. To reduce line drag and make the casting easier, a sinking shooting line is generally used. The class tippet and 100-pound mono shock leader are tied according to IGFA specifications as described in Chapter 1.

All this is fairly standard, but, as you might expect, when it comes to flies for billfish there is considerable variation. Not to offend any tyers, but when a billfish is really lit up the intricacies of a particular pattern are not going to matter much. Bill Barnes has had some abominations devoured quicker than it takes to read this sentence. He thought that the fact that the fly looked so bad might have had something to do with the fish's determination to destroy it. My best advice is to go with Harry Kime's suggestion and tie flies that resemble the particular teaser's size and color. In that regard I generally tie all-white patterns with Mylar and Flashabou for added visibility.

Hooks generally range from 3/0 to 6/0. The gap on the barb should be narrowed to where it is almost flat and the point is filed to a four-sided diamond with razor-edge sharpness. To further assure a positive hookup many anglers are using a tandem hook with the trailing hook riding up. A pattern I developed for offshore use called the Big-Game Fly incorporates an offset-style secondary hook. I use 90-pound Sevenstrand multi-strand wire with size A-3 crimping sleeves to attach the trailing hook; if you are record conscious, be advised that the hook eyes cannot be farther than six inches apart and the second hook may not extend beyond the wing material.

If you try your hand at this facet of the sport, you'll find that big game on fly gear can take on even bigger dimensions.

While there are limitations to the use of fly tackle in saltwater, they have yet to be defined precisely and I hope that you will derive a great deal of your own satisfaction in setting and pursuing your personal goals with the long rod, in helping to develop this exciting brand of fly fishing. Whether you fish for seatrout or sails, mackerel or marlin, the point is to have fun.

As a kid, I saw a poster hanging in a tackle shop that depicted an elated angler holding up his catch. "Fish and feel it," read the caption. I don't think there is any better way of experiencing this than the direct sensations inherent in fly fishing—and the new frontier of saltwater fly fishing has opened tremendously exciting new challenges and opportunities. I invite you to try them.

Bibliography

THE FOLLOWING is a list of publications that provides a variety of different kinds of useful information for saltwater fly fishermen.

Eldridge Tide and Pilot Book, Robert Eldridge White and Marion Jewitt White. This annual publication is a veritable mariner's almanac for the East Coast. It covers everything from tides, currents, and moon phases to fog signals, courses, and distances.

Fishing the Flats, Mark Sosin and Lefty Kreh. New York: Lyons & Burford, Publishers. This is a key source for fly fishermen in shallow-water, tropical tidal flats.

Flies For Saltwater, Dick Stewart and Farrow Allen. North Conway, New Hampshire: Mountain Pond Publishing; distributed by Lyons & Burford, Publishers. This is one of the most extensive reference guides for North American saltwater fly patterns.

Fly Fishing in Salt Water, Lefty Kreh. New York: Lyons & Burford, Publishers. I consider this work to be the bible of saltwater fly fishing.

Inshore Fly Fishing, Lou Tabory. New York: Lyons & Burford, Publishers. Regardless of what coasts you fish, for the shorebound fly fisherman this is an invaluable source book.

Longer Fly Casting, Lefty Kreh. New York: Lyons & Burford, Publishers. The book lives up to its title. All the basic techniques for distance casting are covered by the man who does it best.

Practical Fishing Knots II, Mark Sosin and Lefty Kreh. New York: Lyons & Burford, Publishers. Properly tied connections are the vital links between the fish and the angler and this is the most informative book on the subject.

Salt Water Fly Patterns, Lefty Kreh. Fullerton, California: Maral, Inc. This is an important source for all the major saltwater fly patterns.

Index

Summers, Lawrence, 169–70, 174
surface boils, 78
surf fishing, 45, 77–93; *see also* indiv.
    species, locations
swordfish, 163

Tabory, Lou, *xi, xiii, xiv,* 7, 58, 132,
    133; flies, 53, 88, 99, 104, 106,
    146
tackle, 2; balancing of, 8–10
"tailing," 118
tarpon, 10, 18, 24, 51, 53, 55, 68, 74,
    95, 107, 109, 119–26, 127, 129,
    134, 135, 137, 185
teaser bugs, 154
terns, 166, 167
Texas, 130
tides, 81–82, 87, 90, 107. 108, 112,
    129, 156, 168
Tiemco 800s hooks, 52
tippets, 6, 10, 11, 16, 17, 24, 35, 36,
    144, 145, 147, 163, 167, 197
tournaments, 2; *see also* International
    Game Fish Association
trevally, 57–58, 80
tripletail, 107
trolling, 55, 154–55, 189–90, 195
trout, 2, 53, 106
tuna, 35, 49, 51, 53, 56–57, 68, 76,
    122, 140, 141, 164, 167, 170,

175, 180–85, 192; albacore, 53,
    141, 180, 183; bigeye, 180;
    bluefin, 93, 149, 180; yellowfin,
    5, 35, 48, 49, 53, 70, 72, 141,
    166–67, 180, 183, 188
Tuna Tonic fly, 182–83

undertow, 93

waders, 92
wahoo, 24, 42, 49, 68, 69, 160,
    188–92
wakes, 80
Watt, Jim, 193
wave movements, 83–84, 85, 90, 91,
    93, 168
weakfish, 78, 104–6
weight-forward (WF) lines, 3, 4, 6, 7,
    24, 59, 103
Whistler flies, *xi,* 86, 99, 140, 144
Whitlock Sculpin, 99
Wight, Pete, 178
wind, as factor in fishing, 24, 25, 58,
    90, 129
wire leaders, 36, 39, 41, 42, 103, 134

yellowfin, 5, 35, 48, 49, 53, 70, 72,
    141, 166–67, 180, 183, 188
yellowtail, 78, 93, 149, 151–52, 157

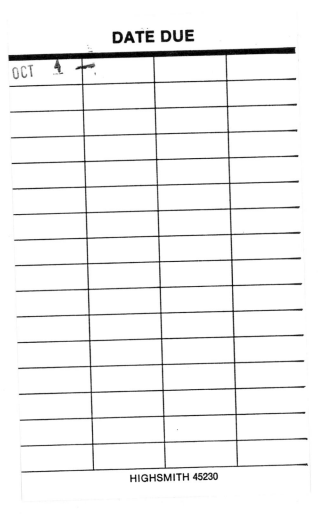

DATE DUE

OCT			

HIGHSMITH 45230